THE RETURN TO HOPI

Published in Denver, CO:

Tuesday – August 13, 2013   Tzolkin – 5: Eagle

6872 E. Iliff Pl.
Denver, CO 80224
SowadiAranjo@gmail.com

Contents

Preface

The Return to Hopi

Leaving at the beginning of this age, traveling east through all world religions to our one heart center has been a journey through the oneness of creation. It was almost eight years ago at the end of a transformational training program that I consciously returned to this journey. At that powerful moment everything thing was as one. These powerful words came through me, "We are creating a world with one heart and soul, HERE AND NOW!" Then on September 14th, 2011 in the oneness of the moment, caught on video and on the nightly news, the falling stars streaking eastward across Turtle Island landed on Hopi. According to numerous eye witnesses, the bright flashing orbs and colorful rays of light of the UFOs caused time to stop, an eternal moment of oneness. As foretold, this day of reconnection was at the crest of the sixth day of the ninth and culminating energy wave of the Mayan (Olmeca/Thoth) Creation Calendar. It was also described as sixth day of creation in the Book of Genesis, as the evolutionary day of humanity. In preparation for the Great Day of Purification, the returning to the heart center of Turtle Island has been is an amazing opportunity, a life altering challenge and a long spiritual journey. Why now? We are in those times of prophecy, in which there will be a series of mega solar storms, ionized coronal mass ejections that will transform all life and consciousness on earth. The U.S. Military's once secret remote viewing program calls this event The Killshot, as the training officer Army Major Ed Dames has recently disclosed. It's interesting to note, according to Major Ed Dames the last sign before the Killshot is the same as the ninth and final sign before the Great Day of Purification. These events will facilitate the purification of modern life on earth and be the catalyst for our evolutionary transformation into the Fifth World. Because of the fall out of the Killshot, the Fifth World may not be experienced here on planet earth. The aftermath of these events are now being deceptively depicted in various Hollywood movies and on numerous TV shows. The ruling elites and their international governmental institutions are preparing their people in their way. How are we preparing ourselves and our communities? It is the intention of this oneness workbook to support us in seeking the truth in our one heart center for these times of evolutionary transformation, the Great Day of Purification.

Sowadi "the falling star" – Tuesday, August 13, 2013

Introduction

Be One in the Shinning Light of God's Creation

Our Seven Days of Creation

Your workbook is an empowering transformational guide to daily live the life of your highest calling. This is your chance to live the life of your dreams. How connected are you to the dreams at your heart center? This workbook has been created to assist you in being one in your highest calling. You will create daily, weekly, 91 day, seven and 100 year intentions to realize your mission here on earth. As the creator of your reality you will empower and harmonize all areas and aspects of your life. Your workbook also includes a 91 day scheduling system to ground your most empowering ways of being. You are the conscious creator of your reality.

Your 91 day scheduling workbook to transform your dreams into reality has been specifically designed for these transformational times. This is your time for greatness! For you it may be to have wealth, health and happiness, experiencing the heaven on earth, or it may be something a little different. What is it for you? What and who is at your loving heart center? This is the time to listen to the transformational voice deep inside of you, calling you to your greatness in the here and now. Your workbook will be both a powerful personal coach and a supportive master guru all in one. Please use it well. You will soon discover aspects about yourself and your current reality which has been preparing you for this important moment. Trusting the source of your inspiration is the key to the guidance you will be receiving.

Congratulations for choosing to be present on planet earth at this historical time. Your conscious participation is urgently required. Together we are living in the transformational times predicted by many ancient cultures and spiritual traditions, from the Hopi Indians of northern Arizona to the Hindus of southern India. Each tradition has prophecies, predications of a future existence, which gives them and now us guidance for these times of prophetic transformation. Listen to the voice inside of you, what is it telling you about these times? The concepts in this guide encourage you to take in all of these traditions, appreciating what they have to offer us in these transformational times. This is an aspect of oneness, to be able to be one with and in all traditions. Does it mean you have to strictly follow or believe in it all? Of course not, it just means to take them in, giving them the light of your day. The idea is to be in the middle of it all, feeling it all informing and guiding you to your highest calling. Eventually you know what is right for you.

In this workbook the word or concept of oneness will be used in the most general terms. What is oneness? First, oneness is unique to your experience. Oneness is at your heart center. You might have experienced the oneness in the beauty of a sunrise or sunset, in the insightful advice of a good friend. Maybe you have had a complete out of body experience of mystical oneness in which you felt the interconnected sacredness in all of life. It has been recently revealed that the daoists masters possess a powerful energy exercise, which facilitates experiencing oneness, creating a state of profound bliss. After thousands of years of persecution the daoist masters have still retained much of the knowledge of how to access and cultivate the universal oneness in life on earth. Their intention is a life of eternity. This workbook will support you in creating a profound transformational awakening through experiencing the interconnected oneness of your life. It is only by you living at the sacred heart center of your life, that the oneness of creation becomes fully realized.

Living from your loving heart, being one in the tree of life, is the deeper and unifying message of Genesis and most indigenous traditions. As the creator of your reality, what intention is at your heart center? Beginning with your clearest intention, your workbook follows the seven day creation process to transform your life, into a oneness way of being. In Chapter 1 you will discover your Oneness Guides to support you throughout your seven days of creation. You will choose to empower your seven days of creation as they build upon each other through the activities of your daily life. It is all about you living at your one heart center. As the delicious conscious fruit of the tree of life, the seventh day of creation grounds your awakened oneness.

By focusing on the seven days of creation, your intentions become one, inspiring your oneness in life on your seventh day of creation. As in Genesis I and the Mayan creation calendar, you choose to be the conscious creator of your reality. At the end of your workbook is your life altering 91 day transformational intention focusing schedule. Your workbook will support you on a daily basis clarify and then manifest your most powerful intentions. Through the power of transformation, this is the time and place for you to live at the one heart center of your life, by living the life of your highest calling.

Monday – Clear the Way. You start your seven day transformational journey by giving it your all, a one-way ticket to sustain the oneness in your heart center. On the first day you will discover your powerful Oneness Guides. You identify the major areas of your life, past and present, and of your surroundings, that deserve your focused loving attention. You clear the deck of your life. As the dutiful janitor of your life, you clean up the lingering debris cluttering the flow of divine wisdom and insight through your life. Even though you might be a little uncertain about revisiting these remote areas of your life, it is the only way to discover the oneness in your heart center. Trusting yourself with certainty is the key. The most challenging step or day is the first one, so consider this to be your launching date - *now* is the time and *here* is the place!

Tuesday - Enliven Dreams. You get to once again connect with and enliven your deepest dreams. Through giving it your all, you have discovered your Transformational Guides to support you in living the life of your highest calling. Your dreams become the colorful burning fire, the guiding lights to your life's heart centered oneness. As with most people your dreams have been safely tucked away and now you have the responsibility to bring them back to the heart center of your life. As you create through living out your dreams, you also give all of your loved ones the opportunity to live their dreams as well. When you enliven and inspire your dreams you are living in the heart centered oneness, the driving force of your inspiring presence on earth.

Wednesday - Inspire Love. You discover how your heart centered love is where the inspiration of life resides. This eternal love is still at the center of your heart and soul. As before, you will once again connect with what causes your heart to skip a mystical beat. You remember what it felt like to experience first love - your body becomes refreshed with the sensations and wisdom of living a life of passion and joy. Through loving your life, your oneness in the tree of life connects you to the passion in your heart centered intentions. By loving all of your life and all of life, this passion and joy inspires the heart centered oneness in your life.

Thursday - Experience Presence. You experience the foundational ways of being which cultivates and creates presence to this sacred moment. Through your complete acceptance of the current reality, you discover how you are able to activate the powers of your Oneness Guides. By being present to your reality and acknowledging what you have created, you accept full responsibility for your life. Through accepting full responsibility, you proceed in your intentional journey to empower the presence of your life, breathing your essence into each moment. Once you activate, accept, appreciate, acknowledge and take full responsibility for your reality, you then experience the wisdom, insight and knowledge of your life. To facilitate breathing your life into this moment, you choose empowering ways of being, to free up and allow the flow of life through your physical and emotional body.

Friday - Ground Wisdom. The wisdom and insight of your life either flows freely into and through you, or it has become constricted throughout your life and body. Thus you are either rowing against the river of life or you are allowing the river of life to flow freely through you, insightfully guiding the way to your one heart center. As you learn to ground all of your ways of being, you will masterfully guide the wisdom of your life. In each moment, the constant interchange of the spirit life is either in harmonious balance or in disharmonious imbalance, and this awareness becomes your masterful wisdom guide. Comprehending and consciously grounding your fundamental, insightful force of life is the next step towards realizing the life of your highest calling.

Saturday - Cultivate Compassion. You inspire your one loving heart center as your most powerful life creator, the synergizing force of your life. Through synergizing with the heart of your life, your heart intentionally beats in communion with all of life.   The intention of your life is be at the intimate intersection of your heart centered oneness, expressed through balancing your **Guiding Values** and **Circle of Life**. By inspiring your heart center, the synergizing force of the universe is able to flow freely through the divine oneness in your life. You are now the conscious creator of your reality. For additional guidance, you begin to create a powerful daily practice to balance, harmonize and then synergize the wisdom and insight into your life.

Sunday – Awaken Oneness. You awaken to your heart centered oneness, being one in creation, evolving your intentions into reality.   Your insightful, intuitive and powerful ways of being are now guiding you in the realization of your **Heart Centered Oneness**. As you are now focused on actualizing your life intention, you experience the oneness in your life. Through being in the oneness of life, you share your dreams, love, presence and insight, and thus inspire your loving heart center. On day seven you now possess the inner acceptance and peace of mind to live as the conscious fruit of the tree of life. As the creator of your reality, all of the previous day's intentions become embodied through your heart centered oneness. You then are able to create a supportive environment to further assist in realizing the life of your highest calling. You expand your earthly impact by breathing life into each sacred moment, standing as the source of universal oneness. As the conscious creator of your life, you step into what is possible through your empowering creative presence.

Chapter 1

Be in the Black,
In the Void Before the Light of the Creator,
The Eternal Beginning of Creation

Monday - Clear the Way

The beginning is the time to be in the black, like an obsidian rock, melting into what *is* and being remade to what is possible. It is important to start where you are at in your journey to realize the life of your highest calling. Please take a few minutes to think about the seven days ahead of you and what is possible when you choose to create a clear intention. To begin your journey, ask yourself which of the following ways of being control or take up any of your thoughts, actions or time. Then circle your four biggest energy consumers.

Fear	Scarcity	Impatience
Worthiness	Closed	Hesitation
Hate	Untrusting	Unfaithful
Doubt	Hopeless	Anger
Lack	Frustration	Arrogance
Depression	Sadness	Regret
Loneliness	Disappointment	Selfishness
Guilt	Disorder	Uncertainty

Which four spirit of life energy consumers did you choose and then circle? Write them down below, left of the arrow.

1. ⟶ _____

2. ⟶ _____

3. ⟶ _____

4. ⟶ _____

Now please take a moment to match each of your energy consumers with their life empowering partner, your empowering Oneness Guides. For instance, anger could be partnered with the spirit giver of compassion, impatience with patience and disappointment with acceptance. What are your most powerful Oneness Guides that you will partner with your past ways of being? Write them below and then above to the right of the arrow.

1.

2.

3.

4.

Sometime today, take a few moments to look up the definition, meaning and history of each of your empowering Oneness Guides. For this important step each of your giving heart ways of being will be your powerful guides directing you toward the life of your highest calling. Know that our evolved humanity and power lies in consciously partnering or balancing all our ways of being, like the balancing or merging of our left and right brain. Today you are transforming your unbalanced ways of being and grounding your spirit of life by empowering your Oneness Guides.

What Are Your Life Altering Events?

If it is later in the day, please take a few moments to refocus so you can to give it your all. Find a safe peaceful location that allows you to relax, maybe on a park bench or possibly at your kitchen table. Once there, take several deep cleansing breaths, breathing in and out all of your surroundings. Close your eyes and remember a life altering event from your youth or past. Go with the first one. Who was involved? What are the images and sounds you see and hear? How do you feel? What do you smell? Where are you located? Give yourself a few moments to experience this event, and while breathing freely write it all down in the space below and on the next page. If you like, draw it as a picture and express it in your words. If necessary use extra paper.

Did you write it all down? If not, then why not? Did you draw a picture of it, and was that easier? How much detail did you give to your life altering event? Did you just go through the motions or did you feel as though you went all the way, giving it your all? In this new moment, you can go deeper by adding even more detail and color.

Do you feel as though you are still holding onto the powerful emotions of this event? If so what can you begin to do now to be one with it, creating a feeling of completion?

As a human on planet earth, you probably have more than one life altering event from your past, so please take a few moments to remember them before you continue on. Begin by listing them here and then at a later date you can go through the same exercise of writing the details of each event on a separate sheet of paper. If you are able to, you can let them go right now, becoming one in them - it's all a choice.

Now that you have completed your life altering event response, ask yourself if you feel like you are completely present. Has it been resolved or are there still lingering issues? Are these events still fresh in your mind with a lot of emotion attached to them? Is it still too difficult to feel them? You have a choice to hold on to these events, blocking the flow of empowering energy through your life or to become one in them. How will you use your Oneness Guides to become one through your life altering events?

The goal is for you to fully accept and appreciate all of your life altering events as necessary for your transformation as an evolved human. What will it take for you to make this happen now? How ready are you to surrender to all of your life experiences?

Is there anything in our current world that is a challenge for you to accept: i.e., pollution, waste, terrorism, war, nuclear power, crime, poverty, violence, injustice, etc.? Write it all down. Are you ready to surrender to them all? Only through fully surrendering to something do you create the power to transform it.

Based on what has happened or what you have not accepted, what beliefs have you made up about yourself or our world? Maybe you don't feel worthy of love, or it is difficult to fully trust people. Notice how connected and similar these are to your past energy consuming ways of being. How will you mindfully use your empowering Oneness Guides to support you in moving through your life altering events and those issues that are a challenge to accept?

1. I will mindfully use _____ to

2. I will mindfully use _____ to

3. I will mindfully use _____ to

4. I will mindfully use _____ to

As you know, your life altering events have been creating emotional and physical blocks, constricting the free flow of the spiritual energy of life through you. How willing are you to break through all that blocks the free flow of life through you?

The goal is for this to be your personal, intention focusing and well used workbook. It is all about you realizing the life of your highest calling. If you think this is being selfish or not worth it, then ask yourself who is this serving or not serving. During the next six days and beyond, your Oneness Guides will be your empowering motivators to inspire your one heart center. Take time each evening to set your intention, becoming one with each of your Oneness Guides.

1. I am _____!

2. I am _____!

3. I am _____!

4. I am _____!

Take a few deep breaths, letting everything go - breathe it all out. You can do this throughout the week, knowing you can control everything through your breath. Take a few moments at the end of each day to skim the next day's intention and questions, to set yourself up for success. It is your intention for it to be a wonderful day tomorrow. Each night, place what you have discovered during the day into your heart and let it rest there throughout the night.

Chapter 2

Enliven Your Dreams, Thinking Outside of the Box
Merging Your Left and Right Brain

Tuesday - Enliven Dreams

1. I am _____!

2. I am _____!

3. I am _____!

4. I am _____!

Today you arise with a bright golden dust in your hands, available to magically enliven the dreams in your heart. Each day take 10-15 minutes in the morning to reflect on your

Oneness Guides, focusing your attention on their power in your life. It is time to once again put your focused attention on your dreams. Now that you have chosen to give it your all by becoming one through your Oneness Guides, today is your special day to dream big again, creating the life of your dreams. Begin the day by imagining all your dreams already true. More important than you writing them down is you imagining your dreams into existence, creating your own personal Disneyland. Take a few deep breaths connecting to this sacred moment, feeling your powerful presence in the moment. Imagine and then start to enliven your dreams in all their rainbow colors and surround sound. What is the biggest dream for your life?

It is about you creating a deep heartfelt connection with your dreams, bringing them into the bright light of each day. Take a few moments to think back and remember what it was like for you as a child. What were and maybe still are your biggest dreams? With whom did you share your dreams? Perhaps it was your brother, mother, father, sister, a family member, best friend or maybe your favorite teddy bear.

At the present moment, how are you living out your dreams, in full color or in black and white? How connected do you feel right now to your heart's deepest dreams?

What are you doing, thinking or saying that is limiting and/or preventing you from living your biggest dreams in 3-D, full color and surround sound?

In this moment, reflect on what are your current dreams in your life. Perhaps it's living in a sustainable community or creating a new business. As added support take a few deep cleansing breaths, feeling your breath travel freely throughout your entire mind, body and soul. Express your dreams as if they already existed in this sacred moment.

How willing and ready are you to continue enlivening and staying deeply connected to your dreams, living the life of your highest calling?

Describe how you will mindfully utilize your empowering Oneness Guides to support yourself in staying deeply connected to and living for your biggest dreams?

As you are enlivening your dreams, imagine the people who might try to discourage you, those who will encourage you the most and those loved ones you hope to inspire to pursue *their* dreams. As you knew when you were young, be mindful with whom and how you share your dreams. Who are your loved ones with whom you do and/or will share your biggest dreams? Imagine them inspired by you living the life of your highest calling.

Over the next five days and into the future, stay heart connected to your dreams, each day envisioning your dreams as already realized. Once again you are will empower your Oneness Guides to assist yourself in enlivening your dreams.

1. I am _____!

2. I am _____!

3. I am _____!

4. I am _____!

Chapter 3

Feel the Loving World,
Dream with Your One Heart and Soul,
In the HERE AND NOW!!!

Wednesday - Inspire Love

1. I am _____!

2. I am _____!

3. I am _____!

4. I am _____!

Today is the day to experience your most loving ways of being through the burning red flames of your first feelings of love. As you begin this wonderful loving day, start by asking yourself, what and who do I love the most in my life?

Take a few deep cleansing breaths and then imagine the powerful feelings of your first true love. Maybe in that eternal moment you lost your breath. What is the insight it provides you to the oneness in your beating heart?

Through breathing in and remembering your first love, it empowers the insightful wisdom at your heart center. Take a few moments to remember those powerful feelings of your first love, maybe it was the big bang of your life. What happened? Who was your first love?

How did you first encounter or meet him or her? Was it at school, on the bus, at student council or maybe on the playground, etc.? How do you still remember that first moment? What were your first feelings, as you are now breathing life into this eternal moment of oneness?

How did you feel in your mind, heart and soul in that moment you met your first love? You can experience those feelings at any moment. What does it feel like?

What is your current connection to your first love? Did you go out with, date, or maybe get married or possibly rejected by him or her? How has this powerful experience affected your love of life?

When you were young, what fun activities, hobbies or interests did you have and always love to do? With whom and how did you manage to do all those wonderful and fun things?

What do you love to do the most right now? How often do you make and/or schedule the time to do what you love to do the most?

What or who inspires you the most or gives you the greatest peace of mind, happiness, joy or jolt of loving energy right now?

To inspire your truest love, start by loving and trusting yourself, knowing that your truest love begins and is sustained at your one heart center. What is your current connection to your heart's truest love?

What is the biggest dream you have which is also your truest love? For example, maybe it is starting a new business, feeding starving children, empowering the people of Haiti or building a sustainable community. What is it for you?

This evening or tonight you can give thanks and praise for this loving day, giving all your dreams to living the life of your highest calling. As you prepare for sleep be assured that your powerful Oneness Guides will support you throughout your journey to the oneness of your loving life.

1. I am _____!

2. I am _____!

3 I am _____!

4 I am _____!

Chapter 4

Experience the Loving Enlightenment of the Maitreya
Being One in the Presence of the 5th Buddha

Thursday - Experience Presence

1. I am _____!

2. I am _____!

3. I am _____!

4. I am _____!

Today is your day to be the loving presence to the deepest green emerald of your life.

Being you are preparing a new start by enlivening your dreams and loving all of your

life, now you get to experience and appreciate the fullness of your life in this present moment. What would it mean for you to fully experience the presence of your life?

In order to expand the presence of your life, which people, situations or circumstances in your life do you have the most difficulty accepting or appreciating? As you know, anything you do not accept continues – or, said another way, what you resist persists.

What would it feel like to surrender to what you have the most difficulty accepting? How will you use your spiritual energy balancing Oneness Guides to accept and then appreciate all that is in your life?

By taking full responsibility for your life, how are you now discovering the deeper meaning of this present moment? How are you appreciating and accepting everything and everyone as they are in this moment?

What areas or loved ones in your life deserve greater acceptance and appreciation?

How will you or do you acknowledge the importance and contributions of all aspects of your life?

When you focus your attention on something or someone you are giving your presence to it or them. Through your loving presence, what are you honoring or giving thanks to on a daily basis?

Through your lack of focused presence, what or who deserves greater honor or giving thanks to in your life?

How are you currently taking full responsibility for everything in your life and this world? What areas of your life and/or our world have you not assumed responsibility for and are now ready and willing to assume responsibility?

How connected was your previous answer to the past question's answer, what you had the most difficulty accepting?

How are you choosing to be present to the powerful oneness of this sacred moment? How does it feel to have presence to the moment?

This is a presence in your life exercise, to *be* in the moment, as you go about your day take deep and regular breaths, connecting your heart center and to all of your surroundings. Then focus on what you have previously lacked presence to in the past. Maybe it is a smile from people walking down the street, seeing birds birched in the trees or hearing the laughter of children playing. Today, take it all in and be present to the difference your presence makes in this world. Then as you end your day, you get to become one through your empowering Oneness Guides.

1. I am _____!

2. I am _____!

3. I am _____!

4. I am _____!

Chapter 5

The Final Mahdi Grounds His Shinning White Horse
Of Service to the Wisdom of Allah's Oneness

Friday - Ground Wisdom

1. I am _____!

2. I am _____!

3. I am _____!

4. I am _____!

Today is your day to cultivate and then share your wisdom by focusing on the powerful white energy of the morning sun. All of the spiritual energy in your life is to be cultivated for the wisdom, insight and guidance it brings into your life. Breathe deeply

in and out, with the freshness of a sun kissed orange, feeling the world in and all around you. By being present, you now possess the ability to deeply breathe in and ground the spiritual energy of life, creating your wisdom to be consciously shared. Take a few moments to feel the energy of the morning or evening sun. What wisdom and guidance are you receiving?

What does it mean for you that all of life is spirit or a form of energy?

Wherever you are at right now, begin by feeling and breathing in the powerful spirit of life that is in and all around you. How are you currently feeling, sensing and experiencing your life as the flow of spiritual energy?

What have been the times or situations in your life that you have felt the spiritual energy of life the most strongly? What were you doing or how were you being to ground this spiritual energy as your life's guiding wisdom?

What will you do now or in the next few days to create the conditions for this renewed level of spiritual energy?

You may start now by staying connected to and focused on your life giving breath as the wisdom of your life. How aware are you during the day to your breath and its guidance of wisdom grounded through your life?

This is a breathing exercise to create the presence to the oneness in this moment. It is best to stand grounded with your feet shoulder length apart and your arms at your side, allowing your body to relax. Close your eyes and take several deep cleansing breaths in, seeing the air come into your body, allowing the air to fill your lungs. Then hold it in for several seconds, feeling your life energy at the top of your head. Opening your eyes let your breath out, feeling it flow from your head down through your body to your feet and then out around you. Try this several times. How does it feel being present to your breath and its life giving wisdom?

As you go about your normal activities, notice your wisdom creating breath. If it is short, practice breathing in and out slowly while noticing everything around you. To take it all in by connecting the energy flow, place the tip of your tongue to the back of your mouth. This will allow the energy to flow, enlightening your pineal gland. To harness your wisdom guiding spiritual energy, know that the nature of spirit is like water, always flowing to where it is most required. Now that you are noticing, feeling and breathing with the spiritual energy of life, what do you sense about the wisdom that is grounded through your life?

As you dedicate 100% of your focused attention to a clear intention how are you harmonizing the spiritual energy in your life?

What are your powerful Oneness Guides, your spiritual energy balancing ways of being? How will you empower your Oneness Guides over the next few days and into the future to realize the life of your highest calling?

1. I will empower _____ by

2. I will empower _____ by

3. I will empower _____ by

4. I will empower _____ by

By constantly grounding your wisdom, through empowering your Oneness Guides, you are now able to balance the spiritual energy through your life. Based on your responses to the previous question, where would your focused attention be of greatest service?

On the next page is the first step in the creation of your **Heart Centered Oneness**. Draw a straight line from the top center to the bottom center and then another line across the circle, thus creating the sacred cross. Where the two lines meet, at your heart center, draw a heart. This is the focal point of your heart centered oneness. Now write your spirit consuming ways of being on one side and their complimentary Oneness Guides on the other side. Thus, through your wisdom, you balance and become one in the spiritual energies of life. As you consciously balance and harmonize your essence you then are able to live the life of your highest calling.

HEART CENTERED ONENESS

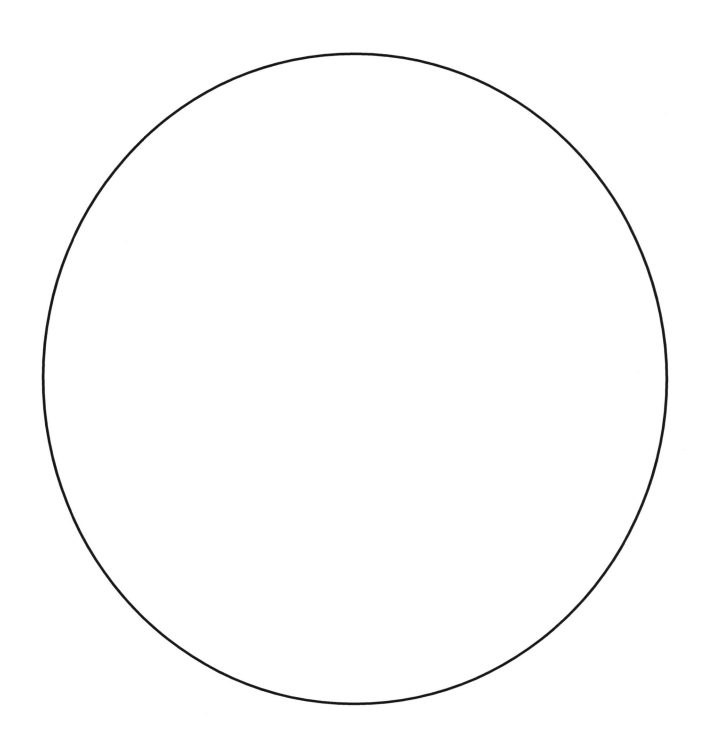

As you complete your **Heart Centered Oneness** over the next two days and into the future, it is important to always stay deeply connected and become one in your wisdom grounding Oneness Guides.

1. I am _____!

2. I am _____!

3. I am _____!

4. I am _____!

Chapter 6

Be One with the Butterflies in Love,
Grounding the Oneness of Adam and Eve

Saturday - Cultivate Compassion

1. I am _____!

2. I am _____!

3. I am _____!

4. I am _____!

Today you cultivate the compassion at your one heart center through enlightening your universe as a bright violet heart. Take a moment to feel the beating of your heart. How

often do you connect, notice and follow the beating guidance of your heart?

What and/or who is at the compassionate heart center of your life? How connected do you presently feel to the heart center of your life?

As you create a clear intention with the guidance of your empowering Oneness Guides, what is still preventing you from living fully in your compassionate heart center?

How are you guided by your heart in making important life decisions? What is a recent example of following the wisdom of your beating heart?

What does it mean for you to harmonize the heart center of your life? How do your loved ones and what is at your heart center give you the greatest opportunity to harmonize your compassionate life?

Guiding Values

To harmonize your life, your Guiding Values are the empowering force, guiding you to realizing the life of your highest calling. Take a moment to reflect on the eight values most important to realizing your compassionate heart center. If you are having a difficulty thinking of eight then ask yourself what qualities do I admire the most in others. As they say, when you spot it you got it.

1.

2.

3.

4.

5.

6.

7.

8.

Guiding Values Grounding

For each of your Guiding Values take a few moments to write at least three ways you do or will ground them in your reality. If compassion is one of your values then for instance you might ground compassion through volunteering at a homeless shelter. Then write a Guiding Value on each of the eight spokes of your **Heart Centered Oneness.**

1. I am _____ by:

   A.

   B.

   C.

2. I am _____ by:

   A.

   B.

   C.

3. I am _____ by:

    A.

    B.

    C.

4. I am _____ by:

    A.

    B.

    C.

5. I am _____ by:

    A.

    B.

    C.

6. I am _____ by:

    A.

    B.

    C.

7. I am _____ by:

    A.

    B.

    C.

8. I am _____ by:

    A.

    B.

    C.

HEART CENTERED ONENESS

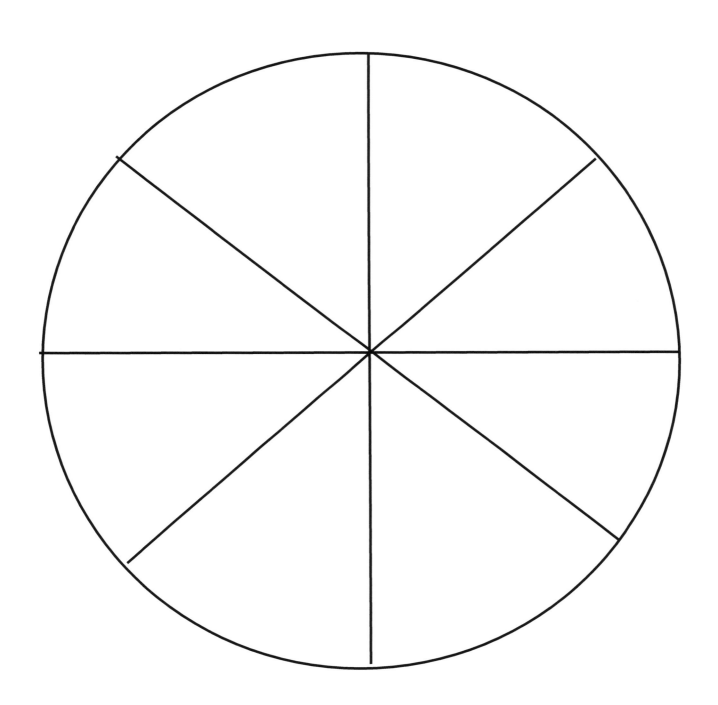

The Circle of Life

The following eight areas or aspects of your life are the foundation to your Circle of Life. For each of the following, start by setting a concise intention and then create a list of three ways you are or will be focusing on each aspect of your Circle of Life. Lastly, write each of your eight aspects on the spokes of your **Heart Centered Oneness**.

1. Community: _____

    A.

    B.

    C.

2. Family: _____

    A.

    B.

    C.

3. Finances: _____

      A.

      B.

      C.

4. Health: _____

      A.

      B.

      C.

5. Recreation: _____

      A.

      B.

      C.

6. Relationships: _____

      A.

      B.

      C.

7. Spirituality: _____

      A.

      B.

      C.

8. Vocation: _____

      A.

      B.

      C.

HEART CENTERED ONENESS

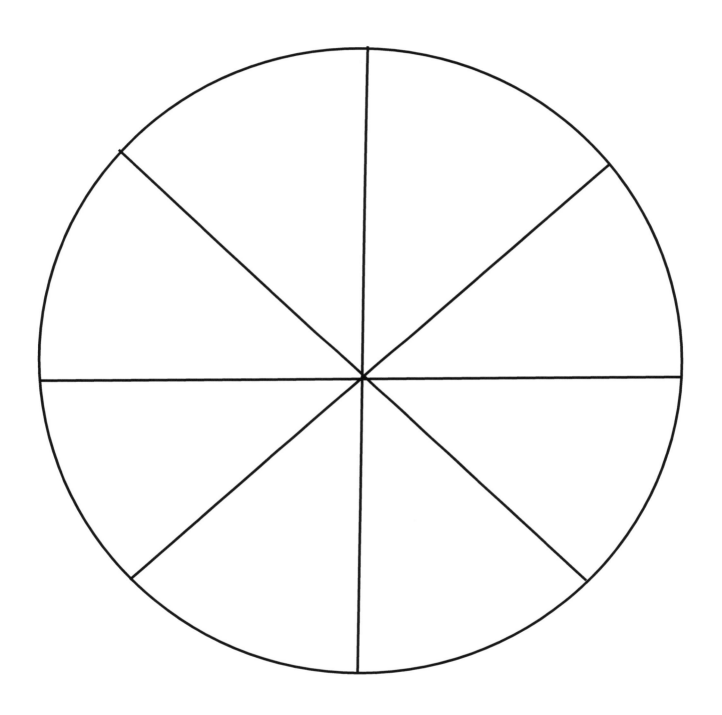

At the end of day six of your transformational journey you are getting closer to your destination, the dawn of the day seven and awaking oneness at your one heart center. As you end your day, once again rest in the loving arms of your compassionate Oneness Guides.

1. I am _____, _____,

_____ and _____ .

Chapter 7

The Light of God Has Just Arrived, Awakening to Oneness
One in God, the Creator of ALL!

Sunday – Awaken Oneness

I am one in _____!

What are you one in? On Sunday, day seven you arise to feel the shining brilliance of a precision cut diamond, inspiring the light across the heart centered oneness of your life. All is perfect, whole and complete. By arriving on the seventh day and getting out of your own way, inspiring the heart of your universe, you are now guided by your Transformational Guides. Awakening to the heart centered oneness of day seven, your powerful Oneness Guides, Guiding Values and your Circle of Life empower the life of your highest calling. Being is the only way to go – being, serving and receiving, as in the eternal tree of life. *Be* your transformational ways, *serve* as your insightful intuition guides you and *receive* the fruits of the tree of life. Sunday is your time for restful reflection, peace of mind and giving thanks for all of your life. At the heart center of your life is the intimate intersection of your transformational ways of being. On the following page write your Guiding Values and Circle of Life aspects on the spokes of your **Heart Centered Oneness**.

HEART CENTERED ONENESS

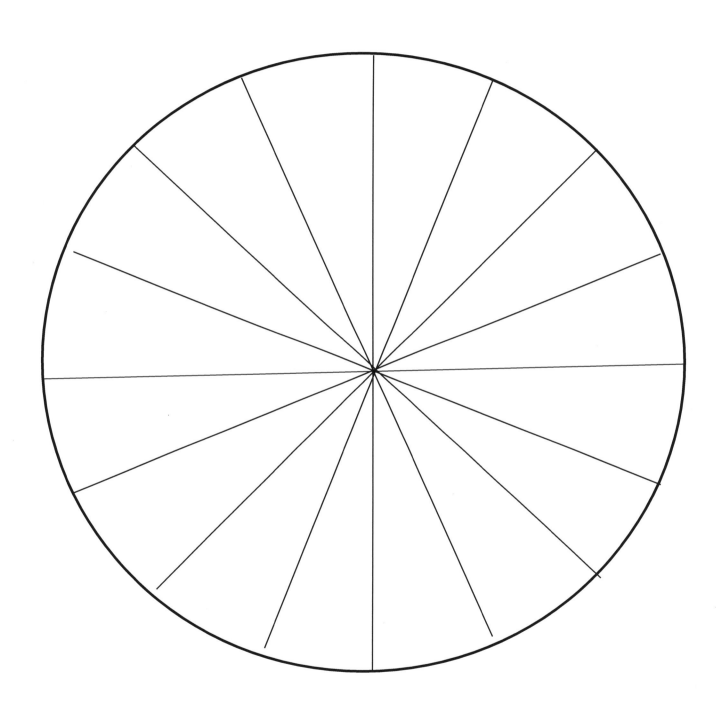

Conclusion

91 Days to Transformation

The intention is for you to consciously transform your ways of being in 91 days, to live the life of your highest calling. An awakening to oneness can happen in a flash of a moment, like a bolt of lightening, maybe at the birth of your child or in a transformational training program. Your awakening, a state of bliss may last for days, or maybe weeks with lingering affects as the years pass. It's as if your transformational genie (VMAT2 gene) decided to come out for a little look and then return back inside the more comfortable lamp. As scientists are recently discovering, activating the pineal gland and the VMAT2 (Vesicular Monoamine Transporter) gene are the keys to us experiencing the eternal oneness in life. The conscious repairing of the VMAT2 gene becomes the vehicle of our evolutionary transformation. According to the research, the VMAT2 gene transports the substances that create our deepest connection to the universe. It is though the regular practice of oneness that the VMAT2 gene stays activated.

An evolutionary transformation is an awakening experience combined with an empowering daily practice. Your daily intention creating practice will keep you focused and energized throughout your transformational journey. It's important to state that it is highly recommended to be vegetarian, vegan and organic if possible, while receiving enough nutrients in your system. Additionally, this is your time to create a simple, light and clean life, shedding all that is weighing you down or draining your precious energy.

Your transformation is both personal and private. It will only be achieved when you decide it is worth your valuable time. Be assured a number of people have been successfully using this transformational process, so it's been fully road tested. Included for your usage are your personal Intention Creation/Scheduling sheets for the next 91 days (13 weeks). This is your intention focusing 91 day opportunity to live the life of your highest calling each moment. As you know 91 days is a long enough time to alter habits, embody and empower your Oneness Guides, Guiding Values and Circle of Life. Additionally, the number 13 (weeks) is the carrier of the powerful creation energies, as in Genesis 1 and the Mayan Creation Calendar, each with seven days and six nights of creation.

Before starting the 91 days, this is a great time to set up a sacred altar, ideally in a private location. It should include what and who is the most import in your life. As the powerful energies of creation begin to flow in and through you, your altar provides a powerful focal point to direct these energies of creation. You will want to focus all of your spiritual energies, through meditation and prayer into realizing the oneness living at your sacred heart center. As you are now becoming one in your intentions, your Oneness Guides continue to lead you to living the life of your highest calling, which is cultivated over time.

As you prepare for the next 91 days, you hopefully have allowed yourself some time to become clear on your intentions. As you are now clear as to what and who are at your heart center. You are balancing, harmonizing and becoming one in your life through empowering your Oneness Guides. Now that you are ready for your intentional journey, start by completing your Week 1 Guiding Intentions sheet. Imagine how you will embody and become one through each of your Oneness Guides, Guiding Values and Circle of Life. Each day begin by reviewing and meditating on your Guiding Intentions. Each week you will have the opportunity to revise your Guiding Intentions. Once you have completed your Guiding Intentions you are ready for day one of your 91 day transformational journey. On the first day of each week you will complete your Intentional Creation sheet for the week. This is your time specific life altering intention. Each day you will have the opportunity to create a new Daily Intention (i.e. Monday – Clear the Way) as part of your Daily Creation. Most importantly each day you will create your Daily Schedule, your daily what by when. For the first several weeks it is highly recommended that you daily review and revise your Seven Days of Creation questions and answers.

At first, it might sound a little challenging, although after several weeks it will all become second nature to you. This is your time and place to inspire the life of your highest calling. It is in the here and now that you create an intentional reality for you and all your loved ones. As you choose to live the life of your highest calling, the oneness of life is realized in and through you.

GUIDING INTENTIONS – WEEK 1

Oneness Guides – I am:

1.

2.

3.

4.

Guiding Values – I am:

1.

2.

3.

4.

5.

6.

7.

8.

Circle of Life – I am:

1.

2.

3.

4.

5.

6.

7.

8.

INTENTIONAL CREATION

My One Week Intention is to:

The What?

By When?

My 91 Day Intention is to:

The What?

By When?

My Seven Year Intention is to:

The What?

By When?

My 100 Year Intention is to:

The What?

By When?

DAILY CREATION

Today's Date:

Day's Intention:

My Focused Attention: _____ to _____

Today's Most Powerful Insights:

1.

2.

3.

What: By When:

1.

2.

3.

4.

5.

6.

7.

8.

9.

10.

Honest Reflection:

Today's Transformation:

DAILY SCHEDULE

Tzolkin: _____ Day _____

Oneness Guides – I am: _____

_____

7:00 A.M.

8:00 A.M.

9:00 A.M.

10:00 A.M.

11:00 A.M.

12:00 P.M.

1:00 P.M.

2:00 P.M.

3:00 P.M.

4:00 P.M.

5:00 P.M.

6:00 P.M

7:00 P.M.

8:00 P.M.

9:00 P.M.

10:00 P.M.

DAILY CREATION

Today's Date:

Day's Intention:

My Focused Attention: _____ to _____

Today's Most Powerful Insights:

1.

2.

3.

What: By When:

1.

2.

3.

4.

5.

6.

7.

8.

9.

10.

Honest Reflection:

Today's Transformation:

DAILY SCHEDULE

Tzolkin: _____ Day _____

Oneness Guides – I am: _____

_____

7:00 A.M.

8:00 A.M.

9:00 A.M.

10:00 A.M.

11:00 A.M.

12:00 P.M.

1:00 P.M.

2:00 P.M.

3:00 P.M.

4:00 P.M.

5:00 P.M.

6:00 P.M

7:00 P.M.

8:00 P.M.

9:00 P.M.

10:00 P.M.

DAILY CREATION

Today's Date:

Day's Intention:

My Focused Attention: _____ to _____

Today's Most Powerful Insights:

1.

2.

3.

What: By When:

1.

2.

3.

4.

5.

6.

7.

8.

9.

10.

Honest Reflection:

Today's Transformation:

DAILY SCHEDULE

Tzolkin: _____ Day _____

Oneness Guides – I am: _____

_____

7:00 A.M.

8:00 A.M.

9:00 A.M.

10:00 A.M.

11:00 A.M.

12:00 P.M.

1:00 P.M.

2:00 P.M.

3:00 P.M.

4:00 P.M.

5:00 P.M.

6:00 P.M

7:00 P.M.

8:00 P.M.

9:00 P.M.

10:00 P.M.

DAILY CREATION

Today's Date:

Day's Intention:

My Focused Attention: _____ to _____

Today's Most Powerful Insights:

1.

2.

3.

What: By When:

1.

2.

3.

4.

5.

6.

7.

8.

9.

10.

Honest Reflection:

Today's Transformation:

DAILY SCHEDULE

Tzolkin: _____ Day _____

Oneness Guides – I am: _____

_____

7:00 A.M.

8:00 A.M.

9:00 A.M.

10:00 A.M.

11:00 A.M.

12:00 P.M.

1:00 P.M.

2:00 P.M.

3:00 P.M.

4:00 P.M.

5:00 P.M.

6:00 P.M

7:00 P.M.

8:00 P.M.

9:00 P.M.

10:00 P.M.

DAILY CREATION

Today's Date:

Day's Intention:

My Focused Attention: _____ to _____

Today's Most Powerful Insights:

1.

2.

3.

What: By When:

1.

2.

3.

4.

5.

6.

7.

8.

9.

10.

Honest Reflection:

Today's Transformation:

DAILY SCHEDULE

Tzolkin: _____ Day _____

Oneness Guides – I am: _____

_____

7:00 A.M.

8:00 A.M.

9:00 A.M.

10:00 A.M.

11:00 A.M.

12:00 P.M.

1:00 P.M.

2:00 P.M.

3:00 P.M.

4:00 P.M.

5:00 P.M.

6:00 P.M

7:00 P.M.

8:00 P.M.

9:00 P.M.

10:00 P.M.

DAILY CREATION

Today's Date:

Day's Intention:

My Focused Attention: _____ to _____

Today's Most Powerful Insights:

1.

2.

3.

What: By When:

1.

2.

3.

4.

5.

6.

7.

8.

9.

10.

Honest Reflection:

Today's Transformation:

DAILY SCHEDULE

Tzolkin: _____ Day _____

Oneness Guides – I am: _____

_____

7:00 A.M.

8:00 A.M.

9:00 A.M.

10:00 A.M.

11:00 A.M.

12:00 P.M.

1:00 P.M.

2:00 P.M.

3:00 P.M.

4:00 P.M.

5:00 P.M.

6:00 P.M

7:00 P.M.

8:00 P.M.

9:00 P.M.

10:00 P.M.

DAILY CREATION

Today's Date:

Day's Intention:

My Focused Attention: _____ to _____

Today's Most Powerful Insights:

1.

2.

3.

What: By When:

1.

2.

3.

4.

5.

6.

7.

8.

9.

10.

Honest Reflection:

Today's Transformation:

DAILY SCHEDULE

Tzolkin: _____ Day _____

Oneness Guides – I am: _____

_____

7:00 A.M.

8:00 A.M.

9:00 A.M.

10:00 A.M.

11:00 A.M.

12:00 P.M.

1:00 P.M.

2:00 P.M.

3:00 P.M.

4:00 P.M.

5:00 P.M.

6:00 P.M

7:00 P.M.

8:00 P.M.

9:00 P.M.

10:00 P.M.

GUIDING INTENTIONS – WEEK 2

Oneness Guides – I am:

1.

2.

3.

4.

Guiding Values – I am:

1.

2.

3.

4.

5.

6.

7.

8.

Circle of Life – I am:

1.

2.

3.

4.

5.

6.

7.

8.

INTENTIONAL CREATION

My One Week Intention is to:

The What?

By When?

My 91 Day Intention is to:

The What?

By When?

My Seven Year Intention is to:

The What?

By When?

My 100 Year Intention is to:

The What?

By When?

DAILY CREATION

Today's Date:

Day's Intention:

My Focused Attention: _____ to _____

Today's Most Powerful Insights:

1.

2.

3.

What: By When:

1.

2.

3.

4.

5.

6.

7.

8.

9.

10.

Honest Reflection:

Today's Transformation:

DAILY SCHEDULE

Tzolkin: _____ Day _____

Oneness Guides – I am: _____

_____

7:00 A.M.

8:00 A.M.

9:00 A.M.

10:00 A.M.

11:00 A.M.

12:00 P.M.

1:00 P.M.

2:00 P.M.

3:00 P.M.

4:00 P.M.

5:00 P.M.

6:00 P.M

7:00 P.M.

8:00 P.M.

9:00 P.M.

10:00 P.M.

DAILY CREATION

Today's Date:

Day's Intention:

My Focused Attention: _____ to _____

Today's Most Powerful Insights:

1.

2.

3.

What: By When:

1.

2.

3.

4.

5.

6.

7.

8.

9.

10.

Honest Reflection:

Today's Transformation:

DAILY SCHEDULE

Tzolkin: _____ Day _____

Oneness Guides – I am: _____

_____

7:00 A.M.

8:00 A.M.

9:00 A.M.

10:00 A.M.

11:00 A.M.

12:00 P.M.

1:00 P.M.

2:00 P.M.

3:00 P.M.

4:00 P.M.

5:00 P.M.

6:00 P.M

7:00 P.M.

8:00 P.M.

9:00 P.M.

10:00 P.M.

DAILY CREATION

Today's Date:

Day's Intention:

My Focused Attention: _____ to _____

Today's Most Powerful Insights:

1.

2.

3.

What: By When:

1.

2.

3.

4.

5.

6.

7.

8.

9.

10.

Honest Reflection:

Today's Transformation:

DAILY SCHEDULE

Tzolkin: _____ Day _____

Oneness Guides – I am: _____

_____

7:00 A.M.

8:00 A.M.

9:00 A.M.

10:00 A.M.

11:00 A.M.

12:00 P.M.

1:00 P.M.

2:00 P.M.

3:00 P.M.

4:00 P.M.

5:00 P.M.

6:00 P.M

7:00 P.M.

8:00 P.M.

9:00 P.M.

10:00 P.M.

DAILY CREATION

Today's Date:

Day's Intention:

My Focused Attention: _____ to _____

Today's Most Powerful Insights:

1.

2.

3.

What: By When:

1.

2.

3.

4.

5.

6.

7.

8.

9.

10.

Honest Reflection:

Today's Transformation:

DAILY SCHEDULE

Tzolkin: _____ Day _____

Oneness Guides – I am: _____

_____

7:00 A.M.

8:00 A.M.

9:00 A.M.

10:00 A.M.

11:00 A.M.

12:00 P.M.

1:00 P.M.

2:00 P.M.

3:00 P.M.

4:00 P.M.

5:00 P.M.

6:00 P.M

7:00 P.M.

8:00 P.M.

9:00 P.M.

10:00 P.M.

DAILY CREATION

Today's Date:

Day's Intention:

My Focused Attention: _____ to _____

Today's Most Powerful Insights:

1.

2.

3.

What: By When:

1.

2.

3.

4.

5.

6.

7.

8.

9.

10.

Honest Reflection:

Today's Transformation:

DAILY SCHEDULE

Tzolkin: _____ Day _____

Oneness Guides – I am: _____

_____

7:00 A.M.

8:00 A.M.

9:00 A.M.

10:00 A.M.

11:00 A.M.

12:00 P.M.

1:00 P.M.

2:00 P.M.

3:00 P.M.

4:00 P.M.

5:00 P.M.

6:00 P.M

7:00 P.M.

8:00 P.M.

9:00 P.M.

10:00 P.M.

DAILY CREATION

Today's Date:

Day's Intention:

My Focused Attention: _____ to _____

Today's Most Powerful Insights:

1.

2.

3.

What: By When:

1.

2.

3.

4.

5.

6.

7.

8.

9.

10.

Honest Reflection:

Today's Transformation:

DAILY SCHEDULE

Tzolkin: _____ Day _____

Oneness Guides – I am: _____

_____

7:00 A.M.

8:00 A.M.

9:00 A.M.

10:00 A.M.

11:00 A.M.

12:00 P.M.

1:00 P.M.

2:00 P.M.

3:00 P.M.

4:00 P.M.

5:00 P.M.

6:00 P.M

7:00 P.M.

8:00 P.M.

9:00 P.M.

10:00 P.M.

DAILY CREATION

Today's Date:

Day's Intention:

My Focused Attention: _____ to _____

Today's Most Powerful Insights:

1.

2.

3.

What: By When:

1.

2.

3.

4.

5.

6.

7.

8.

9.

10.

Honest Reflection:

Today's Transformation:

DAILY SCHEDULE

Tzolkin: _____ Day _____

Oneness Guides – I am: _____

_____

7:00 A.M.

8:00 A.M.

9:00 A.M.

10:00 A.M.

11:00 A.M.

12:00 P.M.

1:00 P.M.

2:00 P.M.

3:00 P.M.

4:00 P.M.

5:00 P.M.

6:00 P.M

7:00 P.M.

8:00 P.M.

9:00 P.M.

10:00 P.M.

GUIDING INTENTIONS – WEEK 3

Oneness Guides – I am:

1.

2.

3.

4.

Guiding Values – I am:

1.

2.

3.

4.

5.

6.

7.

8.

Circle of Life – I am:

1.

2.

3.

4.

5.

6.

7.

8.

INTENTIONAL CREATION

My One Week Intention is to:

The What?

By When?

My 91 Day Intention is to:

The What?

By When?

My Seven Year Intention is to:

The What?

By When?

My 100 Year Intention is to:

The What?

By When?

DAILY CREATION

Today's Date:

Day's Intention:

My Focused Attention: _____ to _____

Today's Most Powerful Insights:

1.

2.

3.

What: By When:

1.

2.

3.

4.

5.

6.

7.

8.

9.

10.

Honest Reflection:

Today's Transformation:

DAILY SCHEDULE

Tzolkin: _____ Day _____

Oneness Guides – I am: _____

_____

7:00 A.M.

8:00 A.M.

9:00 A.M.

10:00 A.M.

11:00 A.M.

12:00 P.M.

1:00 P.M.

2:00 P.M.

3:00 P.M.

4:00 P.M.

5:00 P.M.

6:00 P.M

7:00 P.M.

8:00 P.M.

9:00 P.M.

10:00 P.M.

DAILY CREATION

Today's Date:

Day's Intention:

My Focused Attention: _____ to _____

Today's Most Powerful Insights:

1.

2.

3.

What: By When:

1.

2.

3.

4.

5.

6.

7.

8.

9.

10.

Honest Reflection:

Today's Transformation:

DAILY SCHEDULE

Tzolkin: _____ Day _____

Oneness Guides – I am: _____

_____

7:00 A.M.

8:00 A.M.

9:00 A.M.

10:00 A.M.

11:00 A.M.

12:00 P.M.

1:00 P.M.

2:00 P.M.

3:00 P.M.

4:00 P.M.

5:00 P.M.

6:00 P.M

7:00 P.M.

8:00 P.M.

9:00 P.M.

10:00 P.M.

DAILY CREATION

Today's Date:

Day's Intention:

My Focused Attention: _____ to _____

Today's Most Powerful Insights:

1.

2.

3.

What: By When:

1.

2.

3.

4.

5.

6.

7.

8.

9.

10.

Honest Reflection:

Today's Transformation:

DAILY SCHEDULE

Tzolkin: _____ Day _____

Oneness Guides – I am: _____

_____

7:00 A.M.

8:00 A.M.

9:00 A.M.

10:00 A.M.

11:00 A.M.

12:00 P.M.

1:00 P.M.

2:00 P.M.

3:00 P.M.

4:00 P.M.

5:00 P.M.

6:00 P.M

7:00 P.M.

8:00 P.M.

9:00 P.M.

10:00 P.M.

DAILY CREATION

Today's Date:

Day's Intention:

My Focused Attention: _____ to _____

Today's Most Powerful Insights:

1.

2.

3.

What: By When:

1.

2.

3.

4.

5.

6.

7.

8.

9.

10.

Honest Reflection:

Today's Transformation:

DAILY SCHEDULE

Tzolkin: _____ Day _____

Oneness Guides – I am: _____

_____

7:00 A.M.

8:00 A.M.

9:00 A.M.

10:00 A.M.

11:00 A.M.

12:00 P.M.

1:00 P.M.

2:00 P.M.

3:00 P.M.

4:00 P.M.

5:00 P.M.

6:00 P.M

7:00 P.M.

8:00 P.M.

9:00 P.M.

10:00 P.M.

DAILY CREATION

Today's Date:

Day's Intention:

My Focused Attention: _____ to _____

Today's Most Powerful Insights:

1.

2.

3.

What: By When:

1.

2.

3.

4.

5.

6.

7.

8.

9.

10.

Honest Reflection:

Today's Transformation:

DAILY SCHEDULE

Tzolkin: _____ Day _____

Oneness Guides – I am: _____

_____

7:00 A.M.

8:00 A.M.

9:00 A.M.

10:00 A.M.

11:00 A.M.

12:00 P.M.

1:00 P.M.

2:00 P.M.

3:00 P.M.

4:00 P.M.

5:00 P.M.

6:00 P.M

7:00 P.M.

8:00 P.M.

9:00 P.M.

10:00 P.M.

DAILY CREATION

Today's Date:

Day's Intention:

My Focused Attention: _____ to _____

Today's Most Powerful Insights:

1.

2.

3.

What: By When:

1.

2.

3.

4.

5.

6.

7.

8.

9.

10.

Honest Reflection:

Today's Transformation:

DAILY SCHEDULE

Tzolkin: _____ Day _____

Oneness Guides – I am: _____

_____

7:00 A.M.

8:00 A.M.

9:00 A.M.

10:00 A.M.

11:00 A.M.

12:00 P.M.

1:00 P.M.

2:00 P.M.

3:00 P.M.

4:00 P.M.

5:00 P.M.

6:00 P.M

7:00 P.M.

8:00 P.M.

9:00 P.M.

10:00 P.M.

DAILY CREATION

Today's Date:

Day's Intention:

My Focused Attention: _____ to _____

Today's Most Powerful Insights:

1.

2.

3.

What: By When:

1.

2.

3.

4.

5.

6.

7.

8.

9.

10.

Honest Reflection:

Today's Transformation:

DAILY SCHEDULE

Tzolkin: _____ Day _____

Oneness Guides – I am: _____

_____

7:00 A.M.

8:00 A.M.

9:00 A.M.

10:00 A.M.

11:00 A.M.

12:00 P.M.

1:00 P.M.

2:00 P.M.

3:00 P.M.

4:00 P.M.

5:00 P.M.

6:00 P.M

7:00 P.M.

8:00 P.M.

9:00 P.M.

10:00 P.M.

GUIDING INTENTIONS – WEEK 4

Oneness Guides – I am:

1.

2.

3.

4.

Guiding Values – I am:

1.

2.

3.

4.

5.

6.

7.

8.

Circle of Life – I am:

1.

2.

3.

4.

5.

6.

7.

8.

INTENTIONAL CREATION

My One Week Intention is to:

The What?

By When?

My 91 Day Intention is to:

The What?

By When?

My Seven Year Intention is to:

The What?

By When?

My 100 Year Intention is to:

The What?

By When?

DAILY CREATION

Today's Date:

Day's Intention:

My Focused Attention: _____ to _____

Today's Most Powerful Insights:

1.

2.

3.

What: By When:

1.

2.

3.

4.

5.

6.

7.

8.

9.

10.

Honest Reflection:

Today's Transformation:

DAILY SCHEDULE

Tzolkin: _____ Day _____

Oneness Guides – I am: _____

_____

7:00 A.M.

8:00 A.M.

9:00 A.M.

10:00 A.M.

11:00 A.M.

12:00 P.M.

1:00 P.M.

2:00 P.M.

3:00 P.M.

4:00 P.M.

5:00 P.M.

6:00 P.M

7:00 P.M.

8:00 P.M.

9:00 P.M.

10:00 P.M.

DAILY CREATION

Today's Date:

Day's Intention:

My Focused Attention: _____ to _____

Today's Most Powerful Insights:

1.

2.

3.

What: By When:

1.

2.

3.

4.

5.

6.

7.

8.

9.

10.

Honest Reflection:

Today's Transformation:

DAILY SCHEDULE

Tzolkin: _____ Day _____

Oneness Guides – I am: _____

_____

7:00 A.M.

8:00 A.M.

9:00 A.M.

10:00 A.M.

11:00 A.M.

12:00 P.M.

1:00 P.M.

2:00 P.M.

3:00 P.M.

4:00 P.M.

5:00 P.M.

6:00 P.M

7:00 P.M.

8:00 P.M.

9:00 P.M.

10:00 P.M.

DAILY CREATION

Today's Date:

Day's Intention:

My Focused Attention: _____ to _____

Today's Most Powerful Insights:

1.

2.

3.

What: By When:

1.

2.

3.

4.

5.

6.

7.

8.

9.

10.

Honest Reflection:

Today's Transformation:

DAILY SCHEDULE

Tzolkin: _____ Day _____

Oneness Guides – I am: _____

_____

7:00 A.M.

8:00 A.M.

9:00 A.M.

10:00 A.M.

11:00 A.M.

12:00 P.M.

1:00 P.M.

2:00 P.M.

3:00 P.M.

4:00 P.M.

5:00 P.M.

6:00 P.M

7:00 P.M.

8:00 P.M.

9:00 P.M.

10:00 P.M.

DAILY CREATION

Today's Date:

Day's Intention:

My Focused Attention: _____ to _____

Today's Most Powerful Insights:

1.

2.

3.

What: By When:

1.

2.

3.

4.

5.

6.

7.

8.

9.

10.

Honest Reflection:

Today's Transformation:

DAILY SCHEDULE

Tzolkin: _____ Day _____

Oneness Guides – I am: _____

_____

7:00 A.M.

8:00 A.M.

9:00 A.M.

10:00 A.M.

11:00 A.M.

12:00 P.M.

1:00 P.M.

2:00 P.M.

3:00 P.M.

4:00 P.M.

5:00 P.M.

6:00 P.M

7:00 P.M.

8:00 P.M.

9:00 P.M.

10:00 P.M.

DAILY CREATION

Today's Date:

Day's Intention:

My Focused Attention: _____ to _____

Today's Most Powerful Insights:

1.

2.

3.

What: By When:

1.

2.

3.

4.

5.

6.

7.

8.

9.

10.

Honest Reflection:

Today's Transformation:

DAILY SCHEDULE

Tzolkin: _____ Day _____

Oneness Guides – I am: _____

_____

7:00 A.M.

8:00 A.M.

9:00 A.M.

10:00 A.M.

11:00 A.M.

12:00 P.M.

1:00 P.M.

2:00 P.M.

3:00 P.M.

4:00 P.M.

5:00 P.M.

6:00 P.M

7:00 P.M.

8:00 P.M.

9:00 P.M.

10:00 P.M.

DAILY CREATION

Today's Date:

Day's Intention:

My Focused Attention: _____ to _____

Today's Most Powerful Insights:

1.

2.

3.

What: By When:

1.

2.

3.

4.

5.

6.

7.

8.

9.

10.

Honest Reflection:

Today's Transformation:

DAILY SCHEDULE

Tzolkin: _____ Day _____

Oneness Guides – I am: _____

_____

7:00 A.M.

8:00 A.M.

9:00 A.M.

10:00 A.M.

11:00 A.M.

12:00 P.M.

1:00 P.M.

2:00 P.M.

3:00 P.M.

4:00 P.M.

5:00 P.M.

6:00 P.M

7:00 P.M.

8:00 P.M.

9:00 P.M.

10:00 P.M.

DAILY CREATION

Today's Date:

Day's Intention:

My Focused Attention: _____ to _____

Today's Most Powerful Insights:

1.

2.

3.

What: By When:

1.

2.

3.

4.

5.

6.

7.

8.

9.

10.

Honest Reflection:

Today's Transformation:

DAILY SCHEDULE

Tzolkin: _____ Day _____

Oneness Guides – I am: _____

_____

7:00 A.M.

8:00 A.M.

9:00 A.M.

10:00 A.M.

11:00 A.M.

12:00 P.M.

1:00 P.M.

2:00 P.M.

3:00 P.M.

4:00 P.M.

5:00 P.M.

6:00 P.M

7:00 P.M.

8:00 P.M.

9:00 P.M.

10:00 P.M.

GUIDING INTENTIONS – WEEK 5

Oneness Guides – I am:

1.

2.

3.

4.

Guiding Values – I am:

1.

2.

3.

4.

5.

6.

7.

8.

Circle of Life – I am:

1.

2.

3.

4.

5.

6.

7.

8.

INTENTIONAL CREATION

My One Week Intention is to:

The What?

By When?

My 91 Day Intention is to:

The What?

By When?

My Seven Year Intention is to:

The What?

By When?

My 100 Year Intention is to:

The What?

By When?

DAILY CREATION

Today's Date:

Day's Intention:

My Focused Attention: _____ to _____

Today's Most Powerful Insights:

1.

2.

3.

What: By When:

1.

2.

3.

4.

5.

6.

7.

8.

9.

10.

Honest Reflection:

Today's Transformation:

DAILY SCHEDULE

Tzolkin: _____ Day _____

Oneness Guides – I am: _____

_____

7:00 A.M.

8:00 A.M.

9:00 A.M.

10:00 A.M.

11:00 A.M.

12:00 P.M.

1:00 P.M.

2:00 P.M.

3:00 P.M.

4:00 P.M.

5:00 P.M.

6:00 P.M

7:00 P.M.

8:00 P.M.

9:00 P.M.

10:00 P.M.

DAILY CREATION

Today's Date:

Day's Intention:

My Focused Attention: _____ to _____

Today's Most Powerful Insights:

1.

2.

3.

What: By When:

1.

2.

3.

4.

5.

6.

7.

8.

9.

10.

Honest Reflection:

Today's Transformation:

DAILY SCHEDULE

Tzolkin: _____ Day _____

Oneness Guides – I am: _____

_____

7:00 A.M.

8:00 A.M.

9:00 A.M.

10:00 A.M.

11:00 A.M.

12:00 P.M.

1:00 P.M.

2:00 P.M.

3:00 P.M.

4:00 P.M.

5:00 P.M.

6:00 P.M

7:00 P.M.

8:00 P.M.

9:00 P.M.

10:00 P.M.

DAILY CREATION

Today's Date:

Day's Intention:

My Focused Attention: _____ to _____

Today's Most Powerful Insights:

1.

2.

3.

What: By When:

1.

2.

3.

4.

5.

6.

7.

8.

9.

10.

Honest Reflection:

Today's Transformation:

DAILY SCHEDULE

Tzolkin: _____ Day _____

Oneness Guides – I am: _____

_____

7:00 A.M.

8:00 A.M.

9:00 A.M.

10:00 A.M.

11:00 A.M.

12:00 P.M.

1:00 P.M.

2:00 P.M.

3:00 P.M.

4:00 P.M.

5:00 P.M.

6:00 P.M

7:00 P.M.

8:00 P.M.

9:00 P.M.

10:00 P.M.

DAILY CREATION

Today's Date:

Day's Intention:

My Focused Attention: _____ to _____

Today's Most Powerful Insights:

1.

2.

3.

What: By When:

1.

2.

3.

4.

5.

6.

7.

8.

9.

10.

Honest Reflection:

Today's Transformation:

DAILY SCHEDULE

Tzolkin: _____ Day _____

Oneness Guides – I am: _____

_____

7:00 A.M.

8:00 A.M.

9:00 A.M.

10:00 A.M.

11:00 A.M.

12:00 P.M.

1:00 P.M.

2:00 P.M.

3:00 P.M.

4:00 P.M.

5:00 P.M.

6:00 P.M

7:00 P.M.

8:00 P.M.

9:00 P.M.

10:00 P.M.

DAILY CREATION

Today's Date:

Day's Intention:

My Focused Attention: _____ to _____

Today's Most Powerful Insights:

1.

2.

3.

What: By When:

1.

2.

3.

4.

5.

6.

7.

8.

9.

10.

Honest Reflection:

Today's Transformation:

DAILY SCHEDULE

Tzolkin: _____ Day _____

Oneness Guides – I am: _____

_____

7:00 A.M.

8:00 A.M.

9:00 A.M.

10:00 A.M.

11:00 A.M.

12:00 P.M.

1:00 P.M.

2:00 P.M.

3:00 P.M.

4:00 P.M.

5:00 P.M.

6:00 P.M

7:00 P.M.

8:00 P.M.

9:00 P.M.

10:00 P.M.

DAILY CREATION

Today's Date:

Day's Intention:

My Focused Attention: _____ to _____

Today's Most Powerful Insights:

1.

2.

3.

What: By When:

1.

2.

3.

4.

5.

6.

7.

8.

9.

10.

Honest Reflection:

Today's Transformation:

DAILY SCHEDULE

Tzolkin: _____ Day _____

Oneness Guides – I am: _____

_____

7:00 A.M.

8:00 A.M.

9:00 A.M.

10:00 A.M.

11:00 A.M.

12:00 P.M.

1:00 P.M.

2:00 P.M.

3:00 P.M.

4:00 P.M.

5:00 P.M.

6:00 P.M

7:00 P.M.

8:00 P.M.

9:00 P.M.

10:00 P.M.

DAILY CREATION

Today's Date:

Day's Intention:

My Focused Attention: _____ to _____

Today's Most Powerful Insights:

1.

2.

3.

What: By When:

1.

2.

3.

4.

5.

6.

7.

8.

9.

10.

Honest Reflection:

Today's Transformation:

DAILY SCHEDULE

Tzolkin: _____ Day _____

Oneness Guides – I am: _____

_____

7:00 A.M.

8:00 A.M.

9:00 A.M.

10:00 A.M.

11:00 A.M.

12:00 P.M.

1:00 P.M.

2:00 P.M.

3:00 P.M.

4:00 P.M.

5:00 P.M.

6:00 P.M

7:00 P.M.

8:00 P.M.

9:00 P.M.

10:00 P.M.

GUIDING INTENTIONS – WEEK 6

Oneness Guides – I am:

1.

2.

3.

4.

Guiding Values – I am:

1.

2.

3.

4.

5.

6.

7.

8.

Circle of Life – I am:

1.

2.

3.

4.

5.

6.

7.

8.

INTENTIONAL CREATION

My One Week Intention is to:

The What?

By When?

My 91 Day Intention is to:

The What?

By When?

My Seven Year Intention is to:

The What?

By When?

My 100 Year Intention is to:

The What?

By When?

DAILY CREATION

Today's Date:

Day's Intention:

My Focused Attention: _____ to _____

Today's Most Powerful Insights:

1.

2.

3.

What: By When:

1.

2.

3.

4.

5.

6.

7.

8.

9.

10.

Honest Reflection:

Today's Transformation:

DAILY SCHEDULE

Tzolkin: _____ Day _____

Oneness Guides – I am: _____

_____

7:00 A.M.

8:00 A.M.

9:00 A.M.

10:00 A.M.

11:00 A.M.

12:00 P.M.

1:00 P.M.

2:00 P.M.

3:00 P.M.

4:00 P.M.

5:00 P.M.

6:00 P.M

7:00 P.M.

8:00 P.M.

9:00 P.M.

10:00 P.M.

DAILY CREATION

Today's Date:

Day's Intention:

My Focused Attention: _____ to _____

Today's Most Powerful Insights:

1.

2.

3.

What: By When:

1.

2.

3.

4.

5.

6.

7.

8.

9.

10.

Honest Reflection:

Today's Transformation:

DAILY SCHEDULE

Tzolkin: _____ Day _____

Oneness Guides – I am: _____

_____

7:00 A.M.

8:00 A.M.

9:00 A.M.

10:00 A.M.

11:00 A.M.

12:00 P.M.

1:00 P.M.

2:00 P.M.

3:00 P.M.

4:00 P.M.

5:00 P.M.

6:00 P.M

7:00 P.M.

8:00 P.M.

9:00 P.M.

10:00 P.M.

DAILY CREATION

Today's Date:

Day's Intention:

My Focused Attention: _____ to _____

Today's Most Powerful Insights:

1.

2.

3.

What: By When:

1.

2.

3.

4.

5.

6.

7.

8.

9.

10.

Honest Reflection:

Today's Transformation:

DAILY SCHEDULE

Tzolkin: _____ Day _____

Oneness Guides – I am: _____

_____

7:00 A.M.

8:00 A.M.

9:00 A.M.

10:00 A.M.

11:00 A.M.

12:00 P.M.

1:00 P.M.

2:00 P.M.

3:00 P.M.

4:00 P.M.

5:00 P.M.

6:00 P.M

7:00 P.M.

8:00 P.M.

9:00 P.M.

10:00 P.M.

DAILY CREATION

Today's Date:

Day's Intention:

My Focused Attention: _____ to _____

Today's Most Powerful Insights:

1.

2.

3.

What: By When:

1.

2.

3.

4.

5.

6.

7.

8.

9.

10.

Honest Reflection:

Today's Transformation:

DAILY SCHEDULE

Tzolkin: _____ Day _____

Oneness Guides – I am: _____

_____

7:00 A.M.

8:00 A.M.

9:00 A.M.

10:00 A.M.

11:00 A.M.

12:00 P.M.

1:00 P.M.

2:00 P.M.

3:00 P.M.

4:00 P.M.

5:00 P.M.

6:00 P.M

7:00 P.M.

8:00 P.M.

9:00 P.M.

10:00 P.M.

DAILY CREATION

Today's Date:

Day's Intention:

My Focused Attention: _____ to _____

Today's Most Powerful Insights:

1.

2.

3.

What: By When:

1.

2.

3.

4.

5.

6.

7.

8.

9.

10.

Honest Reflection:

Today's Transformation:

DAILY SCHEDULE

Tzolkin: _____ Day _____

Oneness Guides – I am: _____

_____

7:00 A.M.

8:00 A.M.

9:00 A.M.

10:00 A.M.

11:00 A.M.

12:00 P.M.

1:00 P.M.

2:00 P.M.

3:00 P.M.

4:00 P.M.

5:00 P.M.

6:00 P.M

7:00 P.M.

8:00 P.M.

9:00 P.M.

10:00 P.M.

DAILY CREATION

Today's Date:

Day's Intention:

My Focused Attention: _____ to _____

Today's Most Powerful Insights:

1.

2.

3.

What: By When:

1.

2.

3.

4.

5.

6.

7.

8.

9.

10.

Honest Reflection:

Today's Transformation:

DAILY SCHEDULE

Tzolkin: _____ Day _____

Oneness Guides – I am: _____

_____

7:00 A.M.

8:00 A.M.

9:00 A.M.

10:00 A.M.

11:00 A.M.

12:00 P.M.

1:00 P.M.

2:00 P.M.

3:00 P.M.

4:00 P.M.

5:00 P.M.

6:00 P.M

7:00 P.M.

8:00 P.M.

9:00 P.M.

10:00 P.M.

DAILY CREATION

Today's Date:

Day's Intention:

My Focused Attention: _____ to _____

Today's Most Powerful Insights:

1.

2.

3.

What: By When:

1.

2.

3.

4.

5.

6.

7.

8.

9.

10.

Honest Reflection:

Today's Transformation:

DAILY SCHEDULE

Tzolkin: _____ Day _____

Oneness Guides – I am: _____

_____

7:00 A.M.

8:00 A.M.

9:00 A.M.

10:00 A.M.

11:00 A.M.

12:00 P.M.

1:00 P.M.

2:00 P.M.

3:00 P.M.

4:00 P.M.

5:00 P.M.

6:00 P.M

7:00 P.M.

8:00 P.M.

9:00 P.M.

10:00 P.M.

GUIDING INTENTIONS – WEEK 7

Oneness Guides – I am:

1.

2.

3.

4.

Guiding Values – I am:

1.

2.

3.

4.

5.

6.

7.

8.

Circle of Life – I am:

1.

2.

3.

4.

5.

6.

7.

8.

INTENTIONAL CREATION

My One Week Intention is to:

The What?

By When?

My 91 Day Intention is to:

The What?

By When?

My Seven Year Intention is to:

The What?

By When?

My 100 Year Intention is to:

The What?

By When?

DAILY CREATION

Today's Date:

Day's Intention:

My Focused Attention: _____ to _____

Today's Most Powerful Insights:

1.

2.

3.

What: By When:

1.

2.

3.

4.

5.

6.

7.

8.

9.

10.

Honest Reflection:

Today's Transformation:

DAILY SCHEDULE

Tzolkin: _____ Day _____

Oneness Guides – I am: _____

_____

7:00 A.M.

8:00 A.M.

9:00 A.M.

10:00 A.M.

11:00 A.M.

12:00 P.M.

1:00 P.M.

2:00 P.M.

3:00 P.M.

4:00 P.M.

5:00 P.M.

6:00 P.M

7:00 P.M.

8:00 P.M.

9:00 P.M.

10:00 P.M.

DAILY CREATION

Today's Date:

Day's Intention:

My Focused Attention: _____ to _____

Today's Most Powerful Insights:

1.

2.

3.

What: By When:

1.

2.

3.

4.

5.

6.

7.

8.

9.

10.

Honest Reflection:

Today's Transformation:

DAILY SCHEDULE

Tzolkin: _____ Day _____

Oneness Guides – I am: _____

_____

7:00 A.M.

8:00 A.M.

9:00 A.M.

10:00 A.M.

11:00 A.M.

12:00 P.M.

1:00 P.M.

2:00 P.M.

3:00 P.M.

4:00 P.M.

5:00 P.M.

6:00 P.M

7:00 P.M.

8:00 P.M.

9:00 P.M.

10:00 P.M.

DAILY CREATION

Today's Date:

Day's Intention:

My Focused Attention: _____ to _____

Today's Most Powerful Insights:

1.

2.

3.

What: By When:

1.

2.

3.

4.

5.

6.

7.

8.

9.

10.

Honest Reflection:

Today's Transformation:

DAILY SCHEDULE

Tzolkin: _____ Day _____

Oneness Guides – I am: _____

_____

7:00 A.M.

8:00 A.M.

9:00 A.M.

10:00 A.M.

11:00 A.M.

12:00 P.M.

1:00 P.M.

2:00 P.M.

3:00 P.M.

4:00 P.M.

5:00 P.M.

6:00 P.M

7:00 P.M.

8:00 P.M.

9:00 P.M.

10:00 P.M.

DAILY CREATION

Today's Date:

Day's Intention:

My Focused Attention: _____ to _____

Today's Most Powerful Insights:

1.

2.

3.

What: By When:

1.

2.

3.

4.

5.

6.

7.

8.

9.

10.

Honest Reflection:

Today's Transformation:

DAILY SCHEDULE

Tzolkin: _____ Day _____

Oneness Guides – I am: _____

_____

7:00 A.M.

8:00 A.M.

9:00 A.M.

10:00 A.M.

11:00 A.M.

12:00 P.M.

1:00 P.M.

2:00 P.M.

3:00 P.M.

4:00 P.M.

5:00 P.M.

6:00 P.M

7:00 P.M.

8:00 P.M.

9:00 P.M.

10:00 P.M.

DAILY CREATION

Today's Date:

Day's Intention:

My Focused Attention: _____ to _____

Today's Most Powerful Insights:

1.

2.

3.

What: By When:

1.

2.

3.

4.

5.

6.

7.

8.

9.

10.

Honest Reflection:

Today's Transformation:

DAILY SCHEDULE

Tzolkin: _____ Day _____

Oneness Guides – I am: _____

_____

7:00 A.M.

8:00 A.M.

9:00 A.M.

10:00 A.M.

11:00 A.M.

12:00 P.M.

1:00 P.M.

2:00 P.M.

3:00 P.M.

4:00 P.M.

5:00 P.M.

6:00 P.M

7:00 P.M.

8:00 P.M.

9:00 P.M.

10:00 P.M.

DAILY CREATION

Today's Date:

Day's Intention:

My Focused Attention: _____ to _____

Today's Most Powerful Insights:

1.

2.

3.

What: By When:

1.

2.

3.

4.

5.

6.

7.

8.

9.

10.

Honest Reflection:

Today's Transformation:

DAILY SCHEDULE

Tzolkin: _____   Day _____

Oneness Guides – I am: _____

_____

7:00 A.M.

8:00 A.M.

9:00 A.M.

10:00 A.M.

11:00 A.M.

12:00 P.M.

1:00 P.M.

2:00 P.M.

3:00 P.M.

4:00 P.M.

5:00 P.M.

6:00 P.M

7:00 P.M.

8:00 P.M.

9:00 P.M.

10:00 P.M.

DAILY CREATION

Today's Date:

Day's Intention:

My Focused Attention: _____ to _____

Today's Most Powerful Insights:

1.

2.

3.

What: By When:

1.

2.

3.

4.

5.

6.

7.

8.

9.

10.

Honest Reflection:

Today's Transformation:

DAILY SCHEDULE

Tzolkin: _____ Day _____

Oneness Guides – I am: _____

_____

7:00 A.M.

8:00 A.M.

9:00 A.M.

10:00 A.M.

11:00 A.M.

12:00 P.M.

1:00 P.M.

2:00 P.M.

3:00 P.M.

4:00 P.M.

5:00 P.M.

6:00 P.M

7:00 P.M.

8:00 P.M.

9:00 P.M.

10:00 P.M.

GUIDING INTENTIONS – WEEK 8

Oneness Guides – I am:

1.

2.

3.

4.

Guiding Values – I am:

1.

2.

3.

4.

5.

6.

7.

8.

Circle of Life – I am:

1.

2.

3.

4.

5.

6.

7.

8.

INTENTIONAL CREATION

My One Week Intention is to:

The What?

By When?

My 91 Day Intention is to:

The What?

By When?

My Seven Year Intention is to:

The What?

By When?

My 100 Year Intention is to:

The What?

By When?

DAILY CREATION

Today's Date:

Day's Intention:

My Focused Attention: _____ to _____

Today's Most Powerful Insights:

1.

2.

3.

What: By When:

1.

2.

3.

4.

5.

6.

7.

8.

9.

10.

Honest Reflection:

Today's Transformation:

DAILY SCHEDULE

Tzolkin: _____ Day _____

Oneness Guides – I am: _____

_____

7:00 A.M.

8:00 A.M.

9:00 A.M.

10:00 A.M.

11:00 A.M.

12:00 P.M.

1:00 P.M.

2:00 P.M.

3:00 P.M.

4:00 P.M.

5:00 P.M.

6:00 P.M

7:00 P.M.

8:00 P.M.

9:00 P.M.

10:00 P.M.

DAILY CREATION

Today's Date:

Day's Intention:

My Focused Attention: _____ to _____

Today's Most Powerful Insights:

1.

2.

3.

What: By When:

1.

2.

3.

4.

5.

6.

7.

8.

9.

10.

Honest Reflection:

Today's Transformation:

DAILY SCHEDULE

Tzolkin: _____ Day _____

Oneness Guides – I am: _____

_____

7:00 A.M.

8:00 A.M.

9:00 A.M.

10:00 A.M.

11:00 A.M.

12:00 P.M.

1:00 P.M.

2:00 P.M.

3:00 P.M.

4:00 P.M.

5:00 P.M.

6:00 P.M

7:00 P.M.

8:00 P.M.

9:00 P.M.

10:00 P.M.

DAILY CREATION

Today's Date:

Day's Intention:

My Focused Attention: _____ to _____

Today's Most Powerful Insights:

1.

2.

3.

What: By When:

1.

2.

3.

4.

5.

6.

7.

8.

9.

10.

Honest Reflection:

Today's Transformation:

DAILY SCHEDULE

Tzolkin: _____ Day _____

Oneness Guides – I am: _____

_____

7:00 A.M.

8:00 A.M.

9:00 A.M.

10:00 A.M.

11:00 A.M.

12:00 P.M.

1:00 P.M.

2:00 P.M.

3:00 P.M.

4:00 P.M.

5:00 P.M.

6:00 P.M

7:00 P.M.

8:00 P.M.

9:00 P.M.

10:00 P.M.

DAILY CREATION

Today's Date:

Day's Intention:

My Focused Attention: _____ to _____

Today's Most Powerful Insights:

1.

2.

3.

What: By When:

1.

2.

3.

4.

5.

6.

7.

8.

9.

10.

Honest Reflection:

Today's Transformation:

DAILY SCHEDULE

Tzolkin: _____ Day _____

Oneness Guides – I am: _____

_____

7:00 A.M.

8:00 A.M.

9:00 A.M.

10:00 A.M.

11:00 A.M.

12:00 P.M.

1:00 P.M.

2:00 P.M.

3:00 P.M.

4:00 P.M.

5:00 P.M.

6:00 P.M

7:00 P.M.

8:00 P.M.

9:00 P.M.

10:00 P.M.

DAILY CREATION

Today's Date:

Day's Intention:

My Focused Attention: _____ to _____

Today's Most Powerful Insights:

1.

2.

3.

What: By When:

1.

2.

3.

4.

5.

6.

7.

8.

9.

10.

Honest Reflection:

Today's Transformation:

DAILY SCHEDULE

Tzolkin: _____ Day _____

Oneness Guides – I am: _____

_____

7:00 A.M.

8:00 A.M.

9:00 A.M.

10:00 A.M.

11:00 A.M.

12:00 P.M.

1:00 P.M.

2:00 P.M.

3:00 P.M.

4:00 P.M.

5:00 P.M.

6:00 P.M

7:00 P.M.

8:00 P.M.

9:00 P.M.

10:00 P.M.

DAILY CREATION

Today's Date:

Day's Intention:

My Focused Attention: _____ to _____

Today's Most Powerful Insights:

1.

2.

3.

What: By When:

1.

2.

3.

4.

5.

6.

7.

8.

9.

10.

Honest Reflection:

Today's Transformation:

DAILY SCHEDULE

Tzolkin: _____ Day _____

Oneness Guides – I am: _____

_____

7:00 A.M.

8:00 A.M.

9:00 A.M.

10:00 A.M.

11:00 A.M.

12:00 P.M.

1:00 P.M.

2:00 P.M.

3:00 P.M.

4:00 P.M.

5:00 P.M.

6:00 P.M

7:00 P.M.

8:00 P.M.

9:00 P.M.

10:00 P.M.

DAILY CREATION

Today's Date:

Day's Intention:

My Focused Attention: _____ to _____

Today's Most Powerful Insights:

1.

2.

3.

What: By When:

1.

2.

3.

4.

5.

6.

7.

8.

9.

10.

Honest Reflection:

Today's Transformation:

DAILY SCHEDULE

Tzolkin: _____ Day _____

Oneness Guides – I am: _____

_____

7:00 A.M.

8:00 A.M.

9:00 A.M.

10:00 A.M.

11:00 A.M.

12:00 P.M.

1:00 P.M.

2:00 P.M.

3:00 P.M.

4:00 P.M.

5:00 P.M.

6:00 P.M

7:00 P.M.

8:00 P.M.

9:00 P.M.

10:00 P.M.

GUIDING INTENTIONS – WEEK 9

Oneness Guides – I am:

1.

2.

3.

4.

Guiding Values – I am:

1.

2.

3.

4.

5.

6.

7.

8.

Circle of Life – I am:

1.

2.

3.

4.

5.

6.

7.

8.

INTENTIONAL CREATION

My One Week Intention is to:

The What?

By When?

My 91 Day Intention is to:

The What?

By When?

My Seven Year Intention is to:

The What?

By When?

My 100 Year Intention is to:

The What?

By When?

DAILY CREATION

Today's Date:

Day's Intention:

My Focused Attention: _____ to _____

Today's Most Powerful Insights:

1.

2.

3.

What: By When:

1.

2.

3.

4.

5.

6.

7.

8.

9.

10.

Honest Reflection:

Today's Transformation:

DAILY SCHEDULE

Tzolkin: _____ Day _____

Oneness Guides – I am: _____

_____

7:00 A.M.

8:00 A.M.

9:00 A.M.

10:00 A.M.

11:00 A.M.

12:00 P.M.

1:00 P.M.

2:00 P.M.

3:00 P.M.

4:00 P.M.

5:00 P.M.

6:00 P.M

7:00 P.M.

8:00 P.M.

9:00 P.M.

10:00 P.M.

DAILY CREATION

Today's Date:

Day's Intention:

My Focused Attention: _____ to _____

Today's Most Powerful Insights:

1.

2.

3.

What: By When:

1.

2.

3.

4.

5.

6.

7.

8.

9.

10.

Honest Reflection:

Today's Transformation:

DAILY SCHEDULE

Tzolkin: _____ Day _____

Oneness Guides – I am: _____

_____

7:00 A.M.

8:00 A.M.

9:00 A.M.

10:00 A.M.

11:00 A.M.

12:00 P.M.

1:00 P.M.

2:00 P.M.

3:00 P.M.

4:00 P.M.

5:00 P.M.

6:00 P.M

7:00 P.M.

8:00 P.M.

9:00 P.M.

10:00 P.M.

DAILY CREATION

Today's Date:

Day's Intention:

My Focused Attention: _____ to _____

Today's Most Powerful Insights:

1.

2.

3.

What: By When:

1.

2.

3.

4.

5.

6.

7.

8.

9.

10.

Honest Reflection:

Today's Transformation:

DAILY SCHEDULE

Tzolkin: _____ Day _____

Oneness Guides – I am: _____

_____

7:00 A.M.

8:00 A.M.

9:00 A.M.

10:00 A.M.

11:00 A.M.

12:00 P.M.

1:00 P.M.

2:00 P.M.

3:00 P.M.

4:00 P.M.

5:00 P.M.

6:00 P.M

7:00 P.M.

8:00 P.M.

9:00 P.M.

10:00 P.M.

DAILY CREATION

Today's Date:

Day's Intention:

My Focused Attention: _____ to _____

Today's Most Powerful Insights:

1.

2.

3.

What: By When:

1.

2.

3.

4.

5.

6.

7.

8.

9.

10.

Honest Reflection:

Today's Transformation:

DAILY SCHEDULE

Tzolkin: _____ Day _____

Oneness Guides – I am: _____

_____

7:00 A.M.

8:00 A.M.

9:00 A.M.

10:00 A.M.

11:00 A.M.

12:00 P.M.

1:00 P.M.

2:00 P.M.

3:00 P.M.

4:00 P.M.

5:00 P.M.

6:00 P.M

7:00 P.M.

8:00 P.M.

9:00 P.M.

10:00 P.M.

DAILY CREATION

Today's Date:

Day's Intention:

My Focused Attention: _____ to _____

Today's Most Powerful Insights:

1.

2.

3.

What: By When:

1.

2.

3.

4.

5.

6.

7.

8.

9.

10.

Honest Reflection:

Today's Transformation:

DAILY SCHEDULE

Tzolkin: _____ Day _____

Oneness Guides – I am: _____

_____

7:00 A.M.

8:00 A.M.

9:00 A.M.

10:00 A.M.

11:00 A.M.

12:00 P.M.

1:00 P.M.

2:00 P.M.

3:00 P.M.

4:00 P.M.

5:00 P.M.

6:00 P.M

7:00 P.M.

8:00 P.M.

9:00 P.M.

10:00 P.M.

DAILY CREATION

Today's Date:

Day's Intention:

My Focused Attention: _____ to _____

Today's Most Powerful Insights:

1.

2.

3.

What: By When:

1.

2.

3.

4.

5.

6.

7.

8.

9.

10.

Honest Reflection:

Today's Transformation:

DAILY SCHEDULE

Tzolkin: _____ Day _____

Oneness Guides – I am: _____

_____

7:00 A.M.

8:00 A.M.

9:00 A.M.

10:00 A.M.

11:00 A.M.

12:00 P.M.

1:00 P.M.

2:00 P.M.

3:00 P.M.

4:00 P.M.

5:00 P.M.

6:00 P.M

7:00 P.M.

8:00 P.M.

9:00 P.M.

10:00 P.M.

DAILY CREATION

Today's Date:

Day's Intention:

My Focused Attention: _____ to _____

Today's Most Powerful Insights:

1.

2.

3.

What: By When:

1.

2.

3.

4.

5.

6.

7.

8.

9.

10.

Honest Reflection:

Today's Transformation:

DAILY SCHEDULE

Tzolkin: _____ Day _____

Oneness Guides – I am: _____

_____

7:00 A.M.

8:00 A.M.

9:00 A.M.

10:00 A.M.

11:00 A.M.

12:00 P.M.

1:00 P.M.

2:00 P.M.

3:00 P.M.

4:00 P.M.

5:00 P.M.

6:00 P.M

7:00 P.M.

8:00 P.M.

9:00 P.M.

10:00 P.M.

GUIDING INTENTIONS – WEEK 10

Oneness Guides – I am:

1.

2.

3.

4.

Guiding Values – I am:

1.

2.

3.

4.

5.

6.

7.

8.

Circle of Life – I am:

1.

2.

3.

4.

5.

6.

7.

8.

INTENTIONAL CREATION

My One Week Intention is to:

The What?

By When?

My 91 Day Intention is to:

The What?

By When?

My Seven Year Intention is to:

The What?

By When?

My 100 Year Intention is to:

The What?

By When?

DAILY CREATION

Today's Date:

Day's Intention:

My Focused Attention: _____ to _____

Today's Most Powerful Insights:

1.

2.

3.

What: By When:

1.

2.

3.

4.

5.

6.

7.

8.

9.

10.

Honest Reflection:

Today's Transformation:

DAILY SCHEDULE

Tzolkin: _____ Day _____

Oneness Guides – I am: _____

_____

7:00 A.M.

8:00 A.M.

9:00 A.M.

10:00 A.M.

11:00 A.M.

12:00 P.M.

1:00 P.M.

2:00 P.M.

3:00 P.M.

4:00 P.M.

5:00 P.M.

6:00 P.M

7:00 P.M.

8:00 P.M.

9:00 P.M.

10:00 P.M.

DAILY CREATION

Today's Date:

Day's Intention:

My Focused Attention: _____ to _____

Today's Most Powerful Insights:

1.

2.

3.

What: By When:

1.

2.

3.

4.

5.

6.

7.

8.

9.

10.

Honest Reflection:

Today's Transformation:

DAILY SCHEDULE

Tzolkin: _____ Day _____

Oneness Guides – I am: _____

_____

7:00 A.M.

8:00 A.M.

9:00 A.M.

10:00 A.M.

11:00 A.M.

12:00 P.M.

1:00 P.M.

2:00 P.M.

3:00 P.M.

4:00 P.M.

5:00 P.M.

6:00 P.M

7:00 P.M.

8:00 P.M.

9:00 P.M.

10:00 P.M.

DAILY CREATION

Today's Date:

Day's Intention:

My Focused Attention: _____ to _____

Today's Most Powerful Insights:

1.

2.

3.

What: By When:

1.

2.

3.

4.

5.

6.

7.

8.

9.

10.

Honest Reflection:

Today's Transformation:

DAILY SCHEDULE

Tzolkin: _____ Day _____

Oneness Guides – I am: _____

_____

7:00 A.M.

8:00 A.M.

9:00 A.M.

10:00 A.M.

11:00 A.M.

12:00 P.M.

1:00 P.M.

2:00 P.M.

3:00 P.M.

4:00 P.M.

5:00 P.M.

6:00 P.M

7:00 P.M.

8:00 P.M.

9:00 P.M.

10:00 P.M.

DAILY CREATION

Today's Date:

Day's Intention:

My Focused Attention: _____ to _____

Today's Most Powerful Insights:

1.

2.

3.

What: By When:

1.

2.

3.

4.

5.

6.

7.

8.

9.

10.

Honest Reflection:

Today's Transformation:

DAILY SCHEDULE

Tzolkin: _____ Day _____

Oneness Guides – I am: _____

_____

7:00 A.M.

8:00 A.M.

9:00 A.M.

10:00 A.M.

11:00 A.M.

12:00 P.M.

1:00 P.M.

2:00 P.M.

3:00 P.M.

4:00 P.M.

5:00 P.M.

6:00 P.M

7:00 P.M.

8:00 P.M.

9:00 P.M.

10:00 P.M.

DAILY CREATION

Today's Date:

Day's Intention:

My Focused Attention: _____ to _____

Today's Most Powerful Insights:

1.

2.

3.

What: By When:

1.

2.

3.

4.

5.

6.

7.

8.

9.

10.

Honest Reflection:

Today's Transformation:

DAILY SCHEDULE

Tzolkin: _____ Day _____

Oneness Guides – I am: _____

_____

7:00 A.M.

8:00 A.M.

9:00 A.M.

10:00 A.M.

11:00 A.M.

12:00 P.M.

1:00 P.M.

2:00 P.M.

3:00 P.M.

4:00 P.M.

5:00 P.M.

6:00 P.M

7:00 P.M.

8:00 P.M.

9:00 P.M.

10:00 P.M.

DAILY CREATION

Today's Date:

Day's Intention:

My Focused Attention: _____ to _____

Today's Most Powerful Insights:

1.

2.

3.

What: By When:

1.

2.

3.

4.

5.

6.

7.

8.

9.

10.

Honest Reflection:

Today's Transformation:

DAILY SCHEDULE

Tzolkin: _____ Day _____

Oneness Guides – I am: _____

_____

7:00 A.M.

8:00 A.M.

9:00 A.M.

10:00 A.M.

11:00 A.M.

12:00 P.M.

1:00 P.M.

2:00 P.M.

3:00 P.M.

4:00 P.M.

5:00 P.M.

6:00 P.M

7:00 P.M.

8:00 P.M.

9:00 P.M.

10:00 P.M.

DAILY CREATION

Today's Date:

Day's Intention:

My Focused Attention: _____ to _____

Today's Most Powerful Insights:

1.

2.

3.

What: By When:

1.

2.

3.

4.

5.

6.

7.

8.

9.

10.

Honest Reflection:

Today's Transformation:

DAILY SCHEDULE

Tzolkin: _____ Day _____

Oneness Guides – I am: _____

_____

7:00 A.M.

8:00 A.M.

9:00 A.M.

10:00 A.M.

11:00 A.M.

12:00 P.M.

1:00 P.M.

2:00 P.M.

3:00 P.M.

4:00 P.M.

5:00 P.M.

6:00 P.M

7:00 P.M.

8:00 P.M.

9:00 P.M.

10:00 P.M.

GUIDING INTENTIONS – WEEK 11

Oneness Guides – I am:

1.

2.

3.

4.

Guiding Values – I am:

1.

2.

3.

4.

5.

6.

7.

8.

Circle of Life – I am:

1.

2.

3.

4.

5.

6.

7.

8.

INTENTIONAL CREATION

My One Week Intention is to:

The What?

By When?

My 91 Day Intention is to:

The What?

By When?

My Seven Year Intention is to:

The What?

By When?

My 100 Year Intention is to:

The What?

By When?

DAILY CREATION

Today's Date:

Day's Intention:

My Focused Attention: _____ to _____

Today's Most Powerful Insights:

1.

2.

3.

What: By When:

1.

2.

3.

4.

5.

6.

7.

8.

9.

10.

Honest Reflection:

Today's Transformation:

DAILY SCHEDULE

Tzolkin: _____ Day _____

Oneness Guides – I am: _____

_____

7:00 A.M.

8:00 A.M.

9:00 A.M.

10:00 A.M.

11:00 A.M.

12:00 P.M.

1:00 P.M.

2:00 P.M.

3:00 P.M.

4:00 P.M.

5:00 P.M.

6:00 P.M

7:00 P.M.

8:00 P.M.

9:00 P.M.

10:00 P.M.

DAILY CREATION

Today's Date:

Day's Intention:

My Focused Attention: _____ to _____

Today's Most Powerful Insights:

1.

2.

3.

What: By When:

1.

2.

3.

4.

5.

6.

7.

8.

9.

10.

Honest Reflection:

Today's Transformation:

DAILY SCHEDULE

Tzolkin: _____ Day _____

Oneness Guides – I am: _____

_____

7:00 A.M.

8:00 A.M.

9:00 A.M.

10:00 A.M.

11:00 A.M.

12:00 P.M.

1:00 P.M.

2:00 P.M.

3:00 P.M.

4:00 P.M.

5:00 P.M.

6:00 P.M

7:00 P.M.

8:00 P.M.

9:00 P.M.

10:00 P.M.

DAILY CREATION

Today's Date:

Day's Intention:

My Focused Attention: _____ to _____

Today's Most Powerful Insights:

1.

2.

3.

What: By When:

1.

2.

3.

4.

5.

6.

7.

8.

9.

10.

Honest Reflection:

Today's Transformation:

DAILY SCHEDULE

Tzolkin: _____ Day _____

Oneness Guides – I am: _____

_____

7:00 A.M.

8:00 A.M.

9:00 A.M.

10:00 A.M.

11:00 A.M.

12:00 P.M.

1:00 P.M.

2:00 P.M.

3:00 P.M.

4:00 P.M.

5:00 P.M.

6:00 P.M

7:00 P.M.

8:00 P.M.

9:00 P.M.

10:00 P.M.

DAILY CREATION

Today's Date:

Day's Intention:

My Focused Attention: _____ to _____

Today's Most Powerful Insights:

1.

2.

3.

What: By When:

1.

2.

3.

4.

5.

6.

7.

8.

9.

10.

Honest Reflection:

Today's Transformation:

DAILY SCHEDULE

Tzolkin: _____ Day _____

Oneness Guides – I am: _____

_____

7:00 A.M.

8:00 A.M.

9:00 A.M.

10:00 A.M.

11:00 A.M.

12:00 P.M.

1:00 P.M.

2:00 P.M.

3:00 P.M.

4:00 P.M.

5:00 P.M.

6:00 P.M

7:00 P.M.

8:00 P.M.

9:00 P.M.

10:00 P.M.

DAILY CREATION

Today's Date:

Day's Intention:

My Focused Attention: _____ to _____

Today's Most Powerful Insights:

1.

2.

3.

What: By When:

1.

2.

3.

4.

5.

6.

7.

8.

9.

10.

Honest Reflection:

Today's Transformation:

DAILY SCHEDULE

Tzolkin: _____ Day _____

Oneness Guides – I am: _____

_____

7:00 A.M.

8:00 A.M.

9:00 A.M.

10:00 A.M.

11:00 A.M.

12:00 P.M.

1:00 P.M.

2:00 P.M.

3:00 P.M.

4:00 P.M.

5:00 P.M.

6:00 P.M

7:00 P.M.

8:00 P.M.

9:00 P.M.

10:00 P.M.

DAILY CREATION

Today's Date:

Day's Intention:

My Focused Attention: _____ to _____

Today's Most Powerful Insights:

1.

2.

3.

What: By When:

1.

2.

3.

4.

5.

6.

7.

8.

9.

10.

Honest Reflection:

Today's Transformation:

DAILY SCHEDULE

Tzolkin: _____ Day _____

Oneness Guides – I am: _____

_____

7:00 A.M.

8:00 A.M.

9:00 A.M.

10:00 A.M.

11:00 A.M.

12:00 P.M.

1:00 P.M.

2:00 P.M.

3:00 P.M.

4:00 P.M.

5:00 P.M.

6:00 P.M

7:00 P.M.

8:00 P.M.

9:00 P.M.

10:00 P.M.

DAILY CREATION

Today's Date:

Day's Intention:

My Focused Attention: _____ to _____

Today's Most Powerful Insights:

1.

2.

3.

What: By When:

1.

2.

3.

4.

5.

6.

7.

8.

9.

10.

Honest Reflection:

Today's Transformation:

DAILY SCHEDULE

Tzolkin: _____ Day _____

Oneness Guides – I am: _____

_____

7:00 A.M.

8:00 A.M.

9:00 A.M.

10:00 A.M.

11:00 A.M.

12:00 P.M.

1:00 P.M.

2:00 P.M.

3:00 P.M.

4:00 P.M.

5:00 P.M.

6:00 P.M

7:00 P.M.

8:00 P.M.

9:00 P.M.

10:00 P.M.

GUIDING INTENTIONS – WEEK 12

Oneness Guides – I am:

1.

2.

3.

4.

Guiding Values – I am:

1.

2.

3.

4.

5.

6.

7.

8.

Circle of Life – I am:

1.

2.

3.

4.

5.

6.

7.

8.

INTENTIONAL CREATION

My One Week Intention is to:

The What?

By When?

My 91 Day Intention is to:

The What?

By When?

My Seven Year Intention is to:

The What?

By When?

My 100 Year Intention is to:

The What?

By When?

DAILY CREATION

Today's Date:

Day's Intention:

My Focused Attention: _____ to _____

Today's Most Powerful Insights:

1.

2.

3.

What: By When:

1.

2.

3.

4.

5.

6.

7.

8.

9.

10.

Honest Reflection:

Today's Transformation:

DAILY SCHEDULE

Tzolkin: _____ Day _____

Oneness Guides – I am: _____

_____

7:00 A.M.

8:00 A.M.

9:00 A.M.

10:00 A.M.

11:00 A.M.

12:00 P.M.

1:00 P.M.

2:00 P.M.

3:00 P.M.

4:00 P.M.

5:00 P.M.

6:00 P.M

7:00 P.M.

8:00 P.M.

9:00 P.M.

10:00 P.M.

DAILY CREATION

Today's Date:

Day's Intention:

My Focused Attention: _____ to _____

Today's Most Powerful Insights:

1.

2.

3.

What: By When:

1.

2.

3.

4.

5.

6.

7.

8.

9.

10.

Honest Reflection:

Today's Transformation:

DAILY SCHEDULE

Tzolkin: _____ Day _____

Oneness Guides – I am: _____

_____

7:00 A.M.

8:00 A.M.

9:00 A.M.

10:00 A.M.

11:00 A.M.

12:00 P.M.

1:00 P.M.

2:00 P.M.

3:00 P.M.

4:00 P.M.

5:00 P.M.

6:00 P.M

7:00 P.M.

8:00 P.M.

9:00 P.M.

10:00 P.M.

DAILY CREATION

Today's Date:

Day's Intention:

My Focused Attention: _____ to _____

Today's Most Powerful Insights:

1.

2.

3.

What: By When:

1.

2.

3.

4.

5.

6.

7.

8.

9.

10.

Honest Reflection:

Today's Transformation:

DAILY SCHEDULE

Tzolkin: _____ Day _____

Oneness Guides – I am: _____

_____

7:00 A.M.

8:00 A.M.

9:00 A.M.

10:00 A.M.

11:00 A.M.

12:00 P.M.

1:00 P.M.

2:00 P.M.

3:00 P.M.

4:00 P.M.

5:00 P.M.

6:00 P.M

7:00 P.M.

8:00 P.M.

9:00 P.M.

10:00 P.M.

DAILY CREATION

Today's Date:

Day's Intention:

My Focused Attention: _____ to _____

Today's Most Powerful Insights:

1.

2.

3.

What: By When:

1.

2.

3.

4.

5.

6.

7.

8.

9.

10.

Honest Reflection:

Today's Transformation:

DAILY SCHEDULE

Tzolkin: _____ Day _____

Oneness Guides – I am: _____

_____

7:00 A.M.

8:00 A.M.

9:00 A.M.

10:00 A.M.

11:00 A.M.

12:00 P.M.

1:00 P.M.

2:00 P.M.

3:00 P.M.

4:00 P.M.

5:00 P.M.

6:00 P.M

7:00 P.M.

8:00 P.M.

9:00 P.M.

10:00 P.M.

DAILY CREATION

Today's Date:

Day's Intention:

My Focused Attention: _____ to _____

Today's Most Powerful Insights:

1.

2.

3.

What: By When:

1.

2.

3.

4.

5.

6.

7.

8.

9.

10.

Honest Reflection:

Today's Transformation:

DAILY SCHEDULE

Tzolkin: _____ Day _____

Oneness Guides – I am: _____

_____

7:00 A.M.

8:00 A.M.

9:00 A.M.

10:00 A.M.

11:00 A.M.

12:00 P.M.

1:00 P.M.

2:00 P.M.

3:00 P.M.

4:00 P.M.

5:00 P.M.

6:00 P.M

7:00 P.M.

8:00 P.M.

9:00 P.M.

10:00 P.M.

DAILY CREATION

Today's Date:

Day's Intention:

My Focused Attention: _____ to _____

Today's Most Powerful Insights:

1.

2.

3.

What: By When:

1.

2.

3.

4.

5.

6.

7.

8.

9.

10.

Honest Reflection:

Today's Transformation:

DAILY SCHEDULE

Tzolkin: _____ Day _____

Oneness Guides – I am: _____

_____

7:00 A.M.

8:00 A.M.

9:00 A.M.

10:00 A.M.

11:00 A.M.

12:00 P.M.

1:00 P.M.

2:00 P.M.

3:00 P.M.

4:00 P.M.

5:00 P.M.

6:00 P.M

7:00 P.M.

8:00 P.M.

9:00 P.M.

10:00 P.M.

DAILY CREATION

Today's Date:

Day's Intention:

My Focused Attention: _____ to _____

Today's Most Powerful Insights:

1.

2.

3.

What: By When:

1.

2.

3.

4.

5.

6.

7.

8.

9.

10.

Honest Reflection:

Today's Transformation:

DAILY SCHEDULE

Tzolkin: _____ Day _____

Oneness Guides – I am: _____

_____

7:00 A.M.

8:00 A.M.

9:00 A.M.

10:00 A.M.

11:00 A.M.

12:00 P.M.

1:00 P.M.

2:00 P.M.

3:00 P.M.

4:00 P.M.

5:00 P.M.

6:00 P.M

7:00 P.M.

8:00 P.M.

9:00 P.M.

10:00 P.M.

GUIDING INTENTIONS – WEEK 13

Oneness Guides – I am:

1.

2.

3.

4.

Guiding Values – I am:

1.

2.

3.

4.

5.

6.

7.

8.

Circle of Life – I am:

1.

2.

3.

4.

5.

6.

7.

8.

INTENTIONAL CREATION

My One Week Intention is to:

The What?

By When?

My 91 Day Intention is to:

The What?

By When?

My Seven Year Intention is to:

The What?

By When?

My 100 Year Intention is to:

The What?

By When?

DAILY CREATION

Today's Date:

Day's Intention:

My Focused Attention: _____ to _____

Today's Most Powerful Insights:

1.

2.

3.

What: By When:

1.

2.

3.

4.

5.

6.

7.

8.

9.

10.

Honest Reflection:

Today's Transformation:

DAILY SCHEDULE

Tzolkin: _____ Day _____

Oneness Guides – I am: _____

_____

7:00 A.M.

8:00 A.M.

9:00 A.M.

10:00 A.M.

11:00 A.M.

12:00 P.M.

1:00 P.M.

2:00 P.M.

3:00 P.M.

4:00 P.M.

5:00 P.M.

6:00 P.M

7:00 P.M.

8:00 P.M.

9:00 P.M.

10:00 P.M.

DAILY CREATION

Today's Date:

Day's Intention:

My Focused Attention: _____ to _____

Today's Most Powerful Insights:

1.

2.

3.

What: By When:

1.

2.

3.

4.

5.

6.

7.

8.

9.

10.

Honest Reflection:

Today's Transformation:

DAILY SCHEDULE

Tzolkin: _____ Day _____

Oneness Guides – I am: _____

_____

7:00 A.M.

8:00 A.M.

9:00 A.M.

10:00 A.M.

11:00 A.M.

12:00 P.M.

1:00 P.M.

2:00 P.M.

3:00 P.M.

4:00 P.M.

5:00 P.M.

6:00 P.M

7:00 P.M.

8:00 P.M.

9:00 P.M.

10:00 P.M.

DAILY CREATION

Today's Date:

Day's Intention:

My Focused Attention: _____ to _____

Today's Most Powerful Insights:

1.

2.

3.

What: By When:

1.

2.

3.

4.

5.

6.

7.

8.

9.

10.

Honest Reflection:

Today's Transformation:

DAILY SCHEDULE

Tzolkin: _____ Day _____

Oneness Guides – I am: _____

_____

7:00 A.M.

8:00 A.M.

9:00 A.M.

10:00 A.M.

11:00 A.M.

12:00 P.M.

1:00 P.M.

2:00 P.M.

3:00 P.M.

4:00 P.M.

5:00 P.M.

6:00 P.M

7:00 P.M.

8:00 P.M.

9:00 P.M.

10:00 P.M.

DAILY CREATION

Today's Date:

Day's Intention:

My Focused Attention: _____ to _____

Today's Most Powerful Insights:

1.

2.

3.

What: By When:

1.

2.

3.

4.

5.

6.

7.

8.

9.

10.

Honest Reflection:

Today's Transformation:

DAILY SCHEDULE

Tzolkin: _____ Day _____

Oneness Guides – I am: _____

_____

7:00 A.M.

8:00 A.M.

9:00 A.M.

10:00 A.M.

11:00 A.M.

12:00 P.M.

1:00 P.M.

2:00 P.M.

3:00 P.M.

4:00 P.M.

5:00 P.M.

6:00 P.M

7:00 P.M.

8:00 P.M.

9:00 P.M.

10:00 P.M.

DAILY CREATION

Today's Date:

Day's Intention:

My Focused Attention: _____ to _____

Today's Most Powerful Insights:

1.

2.

3.

What: By When:

1.

2.

3.

4.

5.

6.

7.

8.

9.

10.

Honest Reflection:

Today's Transformation:

DAILY SCHEDULE

Tzolkin: _____ Day _____

Oneness Guides – I am: _____

_____

7:00 A.M.

8:00 A.M.

9:00 A.M.

10:00 A.M.

11:00 A.M.

12:00 P.M.

1:00 P.M.

2:00 P.M.

3:00 P.M.

4:00 P.M.

5:00 P.M.

6:00 P.M

7:00 P.M.

8:00 P.M.

9:00 P.M.

10:00 P.M.

DAILY CREATION

Today's Date:

Day's Intention:

My Focused Attention: _____ to _____

Today's Most Powerful Insights:

1.

2.

3.

What: By When:

1.

2.

3.

4.

5.

6.

7.

8.

9.

10.

Honest Reflection:

Today's Transformation:

DAILY SCHEDULE

Tzolkin: _____ Day _____

Oneness Guides – I am: _____

_____

7:00 A.M.

8:00 A.M.

9:00 A.M.

10:00 A.M.

11:00 A.M.

12:00 P.M.

1:00 P.M.

2:00 P.M.

3:00 P.M.

4:00 P.M.

5:00 P.M.

6:00 P.M

7:00 P.M.

8:00 P.M.

9:00 P.M.

10:00 P.M.

DAILY CREATION

Today's Date:

Day's Intention:

My Focused Attention: _____ to _____

Today's Most Powerful Insights:

1.

2.

3.

What: By When:

1.

2.

3.

4.

5.

6.

7.

8.

9.

10.

Honest Reflection:

Today's Transformation:

DAILY SCHEDULE

Tzolkin: _____ Day _____

Oneness Guides – I am: _____

_____

7:00 A.M.

8:00 A.M.

9:00 A.M.

10:00 A.M.

11:00 A.M.

12:00 P.M.

1:00 P.M.

2:00 P.M.

3:00 P.M.

4:00 P.M.

5:00 P.M.

6:00 P.M

7:00 P.M.

8:00 P.M.

9:00 P.M.

10:00 P.M.